boys, guys & men

By Best Selling Author
DIANNE WILSON

boys, guys & men

By Best Selling Author
DIANNE WILSON

BOYS, GUYS & MEN Published by Dianne Wilson
First published in the USA in 2014
Copyright © Dianne Wilson 2014
ISBN 978-0-9840387-2-5

Cover Graphics: Joshua LeGuern.
Typeset in Newport Beach California.
Printed in the USA.
Author Contact Details:
Dianne Wilson
Newport Church PO Box 9577
Newport Beach, CA 92658 USA
Email: dianne.wilson@newportchurch.com
Tel: +1.949.673.1136

design

"God didn't take Eve from Adam's foot that she should be under him, or from his head that she should be above him, but from a rib so that she should be beside him, close to his heart."[1]

Matthew Henry

the author

Dianne is a bestselling author [published by both HarperCollins Australia and Random House Australia] and spokesperson on the issues of body, soul, spirit, healthy living, healthy body image, value and identity. Dianne and her husband Jonathan are the Senior Pastors of Newport Church in Orange County, California. Dianne's entrepreneurial approach to life, and her passionate message of freedom have created a platform for her to help many people. Dianne has devoted her life to seeing people live in freedom and released into all that they were created to be. Born and raised in Sydney, Australia, wife of an amazing husband, mother of many gorgeous children, and grandmother too, Dianne is a passionate church builder – loving God, loving people and loving life! Founding Director of the Imagine Foundation, Dianne has a vision to place a copy of her book Mirror Mirror in the hands of every 9th Grade school girl across the USA.

Other Books by Dianne Wilson:
- ★ GONE – the moment of surrender
- ★ It's Time – leadership & character development
- ★ Body & Soul – a body & soul shaping handbook
- ★ Here To Eternity – a book of hope in seasons of loss
- ★ Mirror Mirror [English and Spanish] – an identity & self-esteem handbook
- ★ Fat Free Forever! – a body shaping handbook
- ★ Back in Shape After Baby – a body shaping handbook
- ★ Fat Free Forever Cookbook – a body shaping cookbook
- ★ Fat Free Forever 101 Tips – a body shaping minibook
- ★ Easy Exercise for Everybody – a body shaping handbook

Lifestyle Courses by Dianne Wilson:
- ★ Mirror Mirror – an identity & self-esteem course
- ★ Body & Soul – a body & soul lifestyle course

"Her heart is full of another world,
even when her hands are most busy about this world."[2]

Matthew Henry

contents

foreword

By Christine Caine
Founder The A21 Campaign

"Mum, can we please go to Aunty Di's house to play with London, and then stay for dinner because Aunty Di cooks the best food!"

My girls ask me this question at least three days a week, and our family plans our Thanksgiving and Christmas vacations around "Aunty Di's" feasts and festivities. I'm so grateful that my kids will have fond memories of home cooked meals, even if they aren't mine! I dearly love Dianne and the entire Wilson clan whom I have known for nearly twenty years.

Dianne and I have walked through much of life's journey together, and I've observed my friend navigate many difficult seasons. Boys, Guys & Men is more than a guide to relationships but also a testimony of amazing grace, unfailing love and relentless tenacity. I'm thrilled that this book made it into your hands because I know it will transform the way you view and do life with those in your world.

This book is an invitation to discover that although our lives are not always perfect and people are not always perfect, our God is perfect, and His love of imperfect people never, ever fails. His mercies are new every morning, and your history does not need to define your destiny. I've sat in courtrooms with Dianne and wept. We've celebrated the births of children and grandchildren, and I've often reminded her that Jesus holds her and her loved ones in the palm of His hands when it seemed like the enemy was prevailing.

Conversely, Dianne has loved our family and my children like her own. She could not have cooked more meals, given more gifts, or lavished more love on my girls if they had come from her own womb. Nick and I would not be able to travel and do so much of what we do around the world if we lacked the strong support system the Wilson family provides, and the way they consistently and graciously open their home.

It is only to an exceptional person like Dianne Wilson that I entrust the care of my most prized possessions on this earth. Perhaps that's the greatest recommendation I can make for a book that covers relationships and identity, marriage, divorce, family, purpose, and Jesus. If you trust someone with your kids, then you can trust what they say to their readers. Dianne not only talks the talk but she also walks the walk, modeling in her life what she shares in this book.

May your life and relationships be greatly enriched because you have read Boys, Guys & Men.

With much love,

Christine Caine

creation

"So God created man in His own image, in the image and likeness of God He created him; male and female He created them."

genesis chapter one verse twenty seven
[amplified version]

introduction

boys guys men

wisdom

"We teach people how to treat us."[1]

Dr. Phil McGraw

This is a book that I wish someone had given me when I was fourteen years old.

Inside each one of us is a desire to find a partner; that one special person who will be our soul mate and with whom we can share the journey of life together.

God does not choose our mate for us. He may have certain people in His mind for us, but ultimately we are the ones who will have to choose our partners in life. We all need wisdom and help in making the right choice, and finding that wisdom is the focus and goal of this book.

My hope is that this book will inspire you to take time to get understanding and apply wisdom in discovering the man of your dreams. We often use terms to describe the person we met who we take an interest in as "the guy that I met" or "the ...boy" or " the ...man."

Is there a difference between boys, guys and men?

a BOY
is a male child; a young man who lacks maturity, judgment, etc.

a GUY
is a friend; a fellow; informal term used for persons of either sex.

a MAN
is an adult male person, as distinguished from a boy or a woman.

The purpose of this book is to explore exactly that, the difference between Boys, Guys and Men. That difference makes all the difference in our relationships. Identifying and understanding that difference are keys to choosing wisely.

This book is divided into three sections:

In Section One, we are going on a journey through my life – True Story.

In Section Two, we are going to explore:
- Ten types of relationships that won't work
- Seven signs that he might be Mr. Wrong
- Five time bombs that may destroy a relationship
- Eight qualities to look for in a life partner
- Chemistry + Call + Construction

In Section Three, we are going to look at the difference between a girl, a chick and a woman, and the part we play in building healthy relationships.

Whether you are a girl, chick or woman, whether you are a boy, guy or man. Whether you are married, single, divorced or widowed. Whether you are a brother or sister, son or daughter, father or mother, husband or wife, my prayer is that you will experience great grace in your relationships, and help others experience great grace too.

Loving someone or finding the "right one" and building a relationship is not easy. It takes trust, commitment, patience, and most importantly, God's grace, to make it work.

When life leaves you feeling like you don't want to play anymore, know that could be your finest moment as you choose to rise up and learn to love again. I once saw a sign above a store that said,

"Work like you don't need the money."

"Dance like nobody's watching."

"Love like you've never been hurt."

I believe God wants us to love and live like we've never been hurt. Negative things happen. Hurts will come, but they don't have to sabotage our future. We have the opportunity to live the rest of our lives like we've never been hurt because of the grace of God. Living like you've never been hurt is not living in denial; it simply means that you can live through the power of God's love in your life.

My story is one about a broken white picket fence that was rebuilt through the power of God's love.

When a man and a woman fall in love and get married, a whole lot of promises are made – called wedding vows. The minister asks the congregation to stand and says to the groom, "Do you take this woman to be your wife? Do you promise to love her, comfort her, honor and protect her, and, forsaking all others, be faithful to her as long as you both shall live?"

And the groom says, "I do."

The minister then says to the bride, "Do you take this man to be your husband? Do you promise to love him, comfort him, honor and protect him, and, forsaking all others, be faithful to him as long as you both shall live?"

The bride says, "I do."

The bride and groom then turn to face each other, as the groom says to the bride, "I take you to be my wife, to have and to hold from this day forward; for better, for worse, for richer, for poorer, in sickness and in health, to love and to cherish, till death us do part, according to God's holy law; and this is my solemn vow."

Likewise, the bride says to the groom, "I take you to be my husband, to have and to hold from this day forward; for better, for worse, for richer, for poorer, in sickness and in health, to love, cherish, and obey till death us do part, according to God's holy law; and this is my solemn vow."

rescued

"God went for the jugular when He sent His own Son. He didn't deal with the problem as something remote and unimportant. In His Son Jesus, He personally took on the human condition, entered the disordered mess of struggling humanity in order to set it right once and for all..."

romans chapter eight
[the message]

They exchange rings and continue to promise each other of their unending love. The minister then pronounces the couple husband and wife, and tells them that they are now married.

He then invites the groom to kiss the bride [ahhh]!

The minister then joins the couple's right hands together and says, "That which God has joined together, let no man divide."

So, what happens when the man who said, "I DO", says "I DON'T anymore"?

What happens when the person who promises to:

Love - then lies.

Comfort - then criticizes.

Honor – then humiliates.

Protect – then inflicts pain.

Forsake all others – then forsakes you.

Be faithful to you as long as you both shall live – then is unfaithful.

Stay with you until death do you part – then leaves you.

What happens when all you want is to live happily ever after?

That's when life all of a sudden does not seem fair. Life becomes messy. However, even though things don't work out the way we expect them to, we don't have to live permanently in the pain and mess of a broken and hurt life.

Life may not be fair, but what is fair is that we can live without the pain of a messy, broken and hurt life. Life can be messy! Father God sent Savior Jesus to rescue us from our messy, broken and hurt lives so that we could start again, new and whole in Him. Whether we caused the pain or whether the pain was inflicted on us, God wants to rescue us and set us on a brand new path for our future.

Redemption.

Choosing to say, "I do" - no matter what, has rebuilt my life.

love

"This is how God showed His love among us: He sent His one and only Son into the world that we might live through Him."

one john chapter four verse nine
[new international version]

Whether you have been through divorce, separation, whether you are single or married – happily or unhappily, you can still say, "I can." "I will." "I do!" This is my creed…

I DO believe:

In the power of the Cross – living from the Cross.

That God is real.

That Jesus loves us all no matter what we've done.

That the Word of God works.

That forgiveness is not optional.

That nothing is too hard for God to fix.

That once you've received God's love you must love others, no matter what they've done.

That everything that happens is either God sent or God used.

That I can live like I've never been hurt.

That the white picket fence can be rebuilt.

Fast forward.

I now have a wonderful husband and six beautiful children. We have his, hers and ours, and we are one big happy family! Step-families don't have to be dysfunctional! I have come to realize that functional families are made up of functional people. I was a Christian when I went through divorce, and I learned that the love of God was what made the difference to me having a life on the other side of divorce. On my wedding day in 1989, 1 Corinthians 13 was read. During my marriage of seven years my faith was strong, my hope was high and even though my marriage ended, love still remains.

The love of God always remains.

Always.

I have one very amazing husband. I love my husband.

I have three incredible sons. I love my sons.

I have three magnificent daughters. I love my daughters.

I also have one very dear ex-husband. I love my ex-husband.

truth

"'Tis strange - but true; for truth is always strange; stranger than fiction; if it could be told, how much would novels gain by the exchange! How differently the world would men behold! How oft would vice and virtue places change! The new world would be nothing to the old, if some Columbus of the moral seas would show mankind their souls' antipodes."[2]

This proverbial saying is attributed to, and coined by, Lord Byron, in a satirical poem Don Juan, 1823

Half my lifetime ago I would observe people.

Couples

Families

Relationships

Happiness.

Peace.

I would observe the qualities of their lives I so desired, but didn't know how to obtain them. I figured that some people were more fortunate than me. I wondered how one changes from a life filled with pain to a life filled with peace. I observed how I could obtain.

I thought there must be a way. Perhaps a space ship I could jump on board, or a magic eraser that could scrub my painful life away. I wondered how someone like me could ever have peace like them.

I just wanted peace.

Peace.

A tranquil state.

Peace.

I found my Peace and His Name is Jesus. He is the Prince of Peace in my life who changed me forever. He helped me deconstruct my mess, and he rebuilt my future. When we allow our Creator room to do what He does best – to make all things new - He lovingly takes the remnants of the mess of our lives and makes a masterpiece of them for our future.

What inspired me to write on the subject of boys, guys and men isn't the pain of a broken marriage. What inspired me is the grace and love of God. He truly makes all things new.

Love.

Never.

Fails.

The end.

risk

"We are afraid to care too much, for fear that the other person does not care at all."[3]

Eleanor Roosevelt

true story

dating

"Dating is a part of the human mating process whereby two people meet socially for companionship, beyond the level of friendship, or with the aim of each assessing the other's suitability as a partner in an intimate relationship or marriage. It can be a form of courtship consisting of social activities done by the couple. While the term has several meanings, it usually refers to the act of meeting and engaging in some mutually agreed upon social activity in public, together, as a couple... Dating as an institution is a relatively recent phenomenon that has mainly emerged in the last few centuries. From the standpoint of anthropology and sociology, dating is linked with other institutions such as marriage and the family which have also been changing rapidly and which have been subject to many forces, including advances in technology and medicine. As humans have evolved from the hunter-gatherers into civilized societies and more recently into modern societies, there have been substantial changes in the relationship between men and women, with perhaps the only biological constant being that both adult women and men must have sexual intercourse for human procreation to happen."[1]

Robert Sapolsky
Biology and Human Behavior: The Neurological Origins of Individuality, 2nd edition [2005].

chapter one

the dating years

dating

dating

dating

Entire seasons of my life were spent, wasted and apparently evaporated in relationships so unhealthy that I became an expert in highly organized dysfunction to try to mask the pain. I thought breaking up with my first boyfriend was the end of the world, and to a thirteen year old it can seem that way. I have many memories of the awkward era of becoming a woman. I was 5'9" by age 14 and felt like a giant. I was insecure and unsure. My parents always spoke kindly to me about me, so my insecurity didn't come from them. I have no brothers and just one sister. My sister is a blonde haired, green-eyed beauty who looks completely different from me. I have very dark brown hair with very dark brown eyes. I used to look at her, and because of our differences, I wished I could be pretty like her. Neither my sister nor I had any experience with boys growing up except for our amazing Dad, a couple of loving uncles and a few great cousins. However, during our teenage years, we both met our fair share of boys, guys and men.

My experiences with some less-than-amazing members of the opposite sex created a picture of boys, guys and men in my mind and my heart. Whether we realize it or not, our life experiences sketch out a mental map by which we navigate through life. Sometimes, we might wonder how we ended up here. Usually, our map – the one sketched out by our life experiences – has quietly shown us the way to our current situation.

I remember one day, as a young teenage girl, I boarded the train on my way home from school, when a guy wearing a long coat sat next to me. I was staring out of the window waiting for my stop to arrive. Looking over to see who had just sat down I was horrified to see him acting in an obscene manner. I was in such deep shock; I couldn't move at first. I was too scared and numb. Eventually, however, I did move past him and once I did, I ran away – very fast and very far away. I ran all the way home. When I arrived home I didn't tell anyone about this experience. I was embarrassed, and for some strange reason, I felt ashamed.

I was one of only a handful of girls in my year who left school still a virgin. I didn't soapbox my values, they were just deeply ingrained in me. During my school years, those values caused me an amazing amount of grief with the opposite sex. The girls who "put out," got taken out. Taken out to parties, to dinner, to fun events and football games. The girls who didn't, somehow earned outcast status. None of this inspired me to change; even when boy after boy, and guy after guy kept telling me that they really wanted to be with me, but couldn't be my boyfriend unless I proved my love for them. This proof of love was physical. I tried to build relationships based on an emotional connection, but it seemed to me that this was the last thing any of these boys and guys wanted. It was physical, or it was terminal, for me.

Not all of my boy and guy friends were just looking for one thing. Many were nice guys, and usually, they traveled in groups, packs, gangs, football teams, classmates.

When I turned sixteen, I thought I had reached relational maturity, so I began dating a guy a few years older than me. I had left school and was now at Business College. I had another boyfriend at the time (as you do when you don't know any better, and when you don't know how to say no...), but really liked this new guy because he was a Christian and his Dad was a Pastor. So I figured that the right thing to do was to break up with the nice guy and date the cool Christian guy. I spent three years of my life from sixteen to nineteen totally devoted to this guy. He was somewhat reciprocal, but for most of our relationship it was me being in love with him and he being preoccupied with himself.

My boyfriend had intimated that intimacy would be the next progressive step in sealing our relationship. I had heard this line before, but this time I was in love and wasn't sure if this is what love does. One day at school I asked my Scripture teacher (who was also my English and History teacher) if I should go ahead and be that close to my boyfriend. I will never forget her response, "If you love him and if you are going to stay together and maybe get married…" I walked away figuring that this must be what love does; that this is what love really looked like. I didn't have anyone telling me it was wrong, I just somehow knew it somehow seemed wrong, for me, for then. I kept thinking back to my Scripture teacher, wondering why she didn't just say it was wrong for my age and stage and that it had the potential to mess me up.

I learned not just the concept of forgiveness from my years of dating this guy, but experienced practicing it as he gave me opportunity after opportunity to forgive him for his inability to remain faithful. He found other girls who would gladly oblige.

He introduced me to the beginning of my get-used-to-it life of relational dysfunction. I learned not to talk to anyone about what I was going through. I learned to carry on regardless.

Too much.

Too young.

I figured that everything would work out eventually. My boyfriend then announced that he was going to make a trip overseas to study at a missions school. I thought this was good news, as it took him away from all the girls who were so readily available to him, and my prayer was that he would focus on his relationship with Jesus. When he left he proclaimed his undying devotion to me and soon after arriving at the missions school, he sent me a beautiful letter proposing to me. He even included a drawing of a ring with a hole cutout so that I could put it on my finger. I was so happy to finally have that commitment from a guy that I had devoted the last three and a half years of my life to.

Fast forward to a year later. The letters stopped coming, and I started wondering. What could it be? This was back in the 1980's, so communication wasn't what it is today. No email, no text, no FaceTime. Nothing but snail mail and phone calls. I made some calls and still couldn't reach my boyfriend. I finally tracked him down and found out why he had stopped writing to me. I learned that he had met another girl, moved in with her family, and he had proposed to her! I was devastated. I couldn't understand what went wrong. What had I done? What was wrong with me? I found out that this new girl was blonde and everything he had been looking for all along, proving (in my mind) how flawed and worthless I was. I thanked him for finally letting me know that after years of undivided devotion.

If it wasn't enough that I sent checks of financial support to help him pay for his schooling and missions work, I was now apparently helping to fund an engagement ring. I stopped sending checks, and I started searching my heart. Getting over this guy took an awfully long time. I had pictured us together forever and had given my heart to him accordingly. I now had many regrets to deal with. It was time now not only to forgive (which I had been well-trained to do) but now I had to learn to forget. This I tried to do by replacement.

So I began dating again, and met another guy. This guy treated me nicely. He was good company, was quite generous, and well, he was just a nice guy. One evening though he let me know that he didn't think we were right for each other and that he wouldn't be coming around anymore. I was so sad, partially because I liked him, but mainly because I was still trying to like myself and this breakup caused me to again ask myself, "Why me?" "What's wrong with me?" I figured I just wasn't good enough. Not pretty enough, not smart enough, not compromised nor compromising enough. After this season, all I knew was just how flawed and worthless I was.

Feelings of worthlessness plagued my soul.

Worthless.

Abandoned.

Empty.

10 KEYS TO DRAMA FREE DATING

1.   **Match your purpose.**
      Purpose is like glue in sealing relationships.

2.   **Live your values.**
      Don't compromise your values now, or you may have to compromise forever.

3.   **Take your time.**
      Spend time together over time. Rush now, regret later.

4.   **Include your friends.**
      Show him your friends, so he can see who you really are. Our friends are, after all, our family of choice.

5.   **Include your family.**
      It's important to include your family, even if they don't agree with your relationship. They may have a perfectly good reason, so don't be afraid to listen up.

6.   **Believe the best.**
      While you are getting to know each other choose to trust and believe the best.

7.   **Communicate openly.**
      Don't hide your feelings now or you may have to hide them later.

8.   **Forgive quickly.**
      Rather than breaking up because of an argument, try forgiving instead.

Forgiveness is essential in any relationship and the sooner you learn to forgive, the more skilled you will become in being a forgiver.

9.   **Be generous.**

Perhaps your partner pays for every meal and outing you go on. Perhaps he doesn't. If it bothers you either way, then talk about. If you are looked after and everything is paid for, then be sure to be generous with words of gratitude. Never feel pressured to "return favors". Gratitude is the appropriate response to genuine generosity.

10.   **Be "ok" to walk away.**

You may be dating, but you aren't married – yet. You may be dating, but you aren't engaged – yet. Dating is meant to be a season of your life where you explore possibilities. If you have no peace, be "ok" to walk away. Do it kindly. Do it calmly. Do it, if you must.

silence

"Nothing strengthens authority so much as silence."[1]

Leonardo da Vinci

chapter two

the silent years

silent

silent

silent

Fast forward to the age of twenty-one. I was doing my best to move forward in all areas of my life: in my career, in my personal life, in serving God in my local church. I was minding my own business and the next thing I know, I was falling in love again with another guy. I tried not to, but he was so kind and complimentary and he loved God, and he appeared to be different. He was from England and had some wonderful family values that seemed a perfect match for me. We began dating, and a few short months later he proposed. I was shocked. I couldn't believe someone wanted to marry me, so I said yes right away! After all, I had no reason to say no. Everything seemed right, and everyone seemed to like him. I then became swept away in wedding planning bliss. There was just one tiny little issue that neither of us had noticed: we didn't actually know each other. From the day we started dating until the day we got married, only six months had passed.

I wonder what would have happened if I would have had the courage to say, "Let's wait so we can get to know each other." I am completely responsible for my insecurity that sealed the deal because I was too scared to say no. I loved him, yes, but I did not know him. I'm not sure if I had waited longer whether that would have helped. It seems that some guys are great when you date them, but then when the chase is over, and they know that they have you for life, that's when you find out who they really are. Some guys open the car door for their lady in one season and then slam it ever after.

Were my parents happy with our decision to get married? Yes, both sets of parents were very happy. No one had any reason to believe what we had wouldn't or couldn't work forever.

Many, many years later, I am still unsure what went wrong or what more I could have done to prepare myself for marriage. I still don't know how I could have fixed what kept breaking in the happily-ever-after life I dreamed of. What I know for sure is that I was young and that once I was married I became isolated. During our honeymoon, we moved abroad to England to be with his family while he applied for a long-term visa to be able to live in my home country. We had no money, so we stayed with his parents in his family home and slept in his old bedroom in two single beds pushed together. We still felt like kids but now we were married.

We were so young.

We were both so naïve.

Young.

Naïve.

Our life together started out full of excitement and adventure, but that excitement, and adventure was short-lived. Soon I became anxious and afraid, I started to realize that my groom could become very angry very quickly very often, over very little. Like a volcano, his internal rage erupted in explosive anger that burned my ears and soul. This anger escalated so fast and so frequently that I couldn't stop it before it happened; I just froze in the midst of the storm.

I was now on the other side of the world, isolated in the company of my new family. I couldn't talk to anyone about it because I was scared and because my new husband had convinced me that I was the problem and the cause of his anger. I knew that we needed help but if I did reach out for help, someone surely would talk to my parents and my Dad would insist I come home. I felt that I couldn't come home as it would hurt too many people. I knew I could forgive and move on, but I wasn't convinced that any of my family and friends could do the same. They would judge him, and they would judge me and I couldn't live with what I couldn't control.

I learned to stay silent.

Silent.

Many years passed, and I had worked out how to stay calm in the middle of these cruel storms. I learned not to run away. I had tried that once, not knowing where to go or what to do, and was immediately brought back home. Home became an interesting word to me. The once safe and happy place of all my childhood years had now become a prison of pain. Crazy outbursts when no one was around were followed by strangely strained silence in the presence of others. I sometimes wondered if I was having a bad dream that was lasting days, weeks, months, years.

But year one passed. We made it. I figured that if we made it through one year alive then we could just keep on going. We moved back to my homeland – Australia – and started to build our lives. I hoped and prayed that everything would change once we arrived back on Aussie soil. After all, this was the place of my happiest memories and where everything was picture perfect. Perhaps going back to England was too much for my husband, I reasoned, and it triggered too much pain from his past.

Truthfully, I still didn't know much about his past. Years of unraveling finally compelled him to share his past with me, and then we had to work out where to file everything. I loved him deeply but didn't know how to help him. I understood that he loved me but that he was unable to help himself. And at all times, I knew as if by secret code, we must remain silent. To find my voice would be to reveal too much pain, both for him and me. Managing the difficult years through silence seemed the best option for two messed up young people who had no idea how to build a healthy relationship.

For the sake of time, and to preserve the relationship that I have worked so hard for more than twenty-five years to rebuild to the point of mutual respect, I won't go into details about those dark years. They were, however, sprinkled with light; because I became a light-maker. I learned to make light in the darkness and make light of the storm. If I hadn't, I might have kissed this life on earth goodbye.

I was just twenty-three years old and had prepared a romantic dinner for two. I had sensed that there was something more-than-usually wrong in our relationship, so I was trying harder than ever to be a good wife. The table set; the candles were lit and my husband arrived home and flopped in his favorite chair. I asked him if he wanted a drink, and he said no. He just stared straight ahead and didn't move. I put on some music – Keith Green. He started to cry, and I asked him what was wrong. He grabbed my hand and pulled me towards him and while still frozen in his pain, told me that he was having an affair with one of his clients.

I don't remember much of that night. I do remember two things: I grabbed our framed wedding photo off the wall and dropped it on the floor. The noise and mess of the shattered glass somehow felt a relief in the midst of the agony I couldn't contain or measure. I couldn't scream, but the shattered glass screamed for me. I ran into my bedroom and sat in the corner pressed up against the wall and the wardrobe. As I sobbed and wailed, rocking back and forth like a baby on the floor, I asked God why.

"Why, Father, didn't you stop him?"

"Why, Father, did this happen?"

"What, Father, did I do to cause this?"

"What, Father, did I do to deserve this?"

Then I realized in that moment of the darkest pain in my life to date, I had a choice: to blame God or to trust God. I loved God with all of my heart. Not only did I know that blaming Him was the wrong thing to do, but I also knew it wasn't God's fault. This affair was my husband's choice – not God's.

He has a free will.

I have a free will.

That evening I chose to trust God, and I have trusted Him at a whole other level since that night, and have never looked back. God is faithful when others are not. That is my ever after story.

I chose to forgive my husband right away. I could see that it would take much longer for him to forgive himself. And every day, from that day on, we each had to work hard to exercise our "forgetory". That was the hard part. I couldn't get this affair out of my head, let alone out of my life. I tried – we tried – and it just took time. I wanted to give our marriage another chance. He wanted the same. We had to work out how to build our future with this experience somehow a part of us, while wishing it could just be behind us. It didn't help when the young woman and her best friend kept calling my home. It didn't help when my husband came home later than he said he would. I developed trust issues I didn't have before, and I didn't know if I would ever be able to trust again. I learned just to deal with it and get on with it and try my best every day to forget about it.

I tried.

Tried.

As time passed, I somehow learned to move on. The only thing that hadn't changed was my husband's habit of becoming quickly and intensely angry. He was happy sometimes, and we genuinely enjoyed those times. But then something I did or said, somewhere I went without his permission or knowledge, set off a sudden cycle of rage that looped on repeat, again and again and again. I didn't mean to make him mad. And speaking honestly, he made me mad too, but that was my problem, not his. Even though it seemed we were drowning in cycles of rage and romance, we were both trying to rebuild our relationship the best way we could.

The two of us included more than us. We were both very close to our families. He included his family in on what happened. I couldn't include mine. His family tried to help. I couldn't bear to think of what my family would say or do. The same silence I used for protection sadly brought questions and bred misunderstanding. One of the inescapable heartaches of a marriage lost is the loss of a family one has come to love. I loved, and still love, his family dearly, although I know they have always found the fact that we ended breaking up a difficult thing to live with. We have all moved on, but I know there is still a remnant of pain for his family who wished we could just get it together and have stayed together.

One day I arrived home from work, and was informed that a member of my husband's family was being sent over to stay with us to help us during this difficult season. That was too much for me. I reached for the telephone to beg that person not to come, but my husband stopped me making that call. He was strong, and I was not. He was angry, and I was scared. He was insisting on my silence, and this was how he enforced it.

That is how he rolled.

That is how we rolled.

I somehow managed to escape with the car keys and quickly sped out of our driveway and down the road. I was driving so fast and crazily that night, so scared he might come after me. I kept my foot on the accelerator and cried out – screamed out – to God to help me. I knew that if I were to hit a telegraph pole that night, it would all be finally over. Relief. I knew that if the police were to catch me, they would lock me up and it would finally be over. Relief. Neither of these things happened. I cried for the pain to stop. Instead, I found myself at the home of the Salvation Army where I curled up, in a ball on the front porch.

I can't recall how and when I ended up going home. I had to straighten out my head before I could arrive. I knew I just needed to toughen up and keep moving on.

Above all I must remain silent.

Silent.

silence

"Your silence gives consent."[1]

Plato

10 KEYS TO SPEAKING UP

1. **Pray.**
   Speak to God first and foremost. Send your complaints His way because He can handle it. Listen to His voice and His direction.

2. **Confide carefully.**
   Be careful who you share your marital problems with, especially if you are hoping for reconciliation.

3. **Choose wisely.**
   Find a professional marriage counselor if you don't have anyone close to you that you would be comfortable talking to.

4. **Include your family.**
   This is essential, albeit difficult. It is the one thing that I wished I had done earlier on in my first marriage. I didn't want my family involved, so I said nothing, but they could have helped me greatly.

5. **Think yourself clear.**
   It can be very difficult to think clearly when life is crazy. Spend time thinking through what is really happening and what you want to see change so that you can communicate cohesively.

6. **Lower your expectations.**
   Lower your expectations of the situation. Don't add pressure to yourself or your spouse while trying to resolve conflict. Use lashings of love at this time.

7. **Raise your tolerance.**
   It is all too easy to add heat to fire when you are living in turmoil. It is a bad habit that will be broken as you choose

to raise your tolerance of your spouse and the situation you are currently trying to resolve.

8.   **Spare your children.**
If you have kids, please spare them the drama and details of your marriage problems, especially if you are working your way out of an abusive relationship. They are not mature enough to handle the sight and sound of the details. They will be old enough one day for you to share your story.

9.   **Lose the heat.**
If you are "over it," you are potentially "boiling over it." Now is not the time to talk. Wait until you are calm and can have a constructive conversation about the need for change.

10.   **Shake off negativity.**
Sometimes you will do everything you can to make things right and yet you still don't see the reconciliation you desire in your relationship. Perhaps you are mistreated and misrepresented on a regular basis. Focus on God and His relationship with you. You are loved.

When you know His Word, you know Him. When you know Him, you know you. When you know you, no one can rob you any more of who you are. To know is to love.

wisdom

"Keep your eyes wide open before marriage, half shut afterwards."[2]

Benjamin Franklin

isolation

"A man who isolates himself seeks his own desire; he rages against all wise judgment."

proverbs chapter eighteen verse one
[new king james version]

chapter three

the baby years
baby
baby
baby

I kept trying to move on.

Trying.

Moving.

On.

I needed a strategy to move on. I was so isolated and therefore would have one-way conversations with myself, trying to work out what to do. I came up with an idea that I honestly felt would help our relationship. I figured the best thing to do would be to have a baby. We had been married for five years, so I figured it was time to start a family. We talked about it, but neither of us felt ready, especially my husband. Nevertheless, I got pregnant right away, and towards the end of my first trimester, lost my baby.

I was devastated.

We were devastated.

I had already decided that I would not blame God for the bad things that happened in my life. He was and is always to be the focus of my trust. But I certainly learned how to blame myself. Like so many women who experience the pain of a miscarriage, I felt like I had caused this loss to happen because of something I had done wrong. My belief system was messed up because my life was messed up. I know now that what happened was not punishment. God does not do that. I also know that I hadn't done anything wrong to deserve that loss. God doesn't do that either. It was just a tragedy without need for blame to be assigned to anyone, except the enemy.

The enemy came to kill steal and destroy.

The sniper.

The deceiver.

The liar.

The mis-guider.

The trouble-maker.

The dream-destroyer.

The enemy is a defeated foe.

Done.

I began to learn more about the pattern of the enemy in my life. I had learned to be so quick to take responsibility for everything that I had completely forgotten about this spiritual adversary who was relentless in his pursuit of my life, my peace, my everything.

I was so sad to lose my baby.

Empty.

Afraid.

Lost.

I kept saying over and over again, "I'm so sorry. I'm so sorry." I felt totally responsible yet had no way of changing anything. I sat on a bench with my Mum outside the hospital room where I had just been discharged. I was teary, and feeling lost. My Mum encouraged me by saying that we would sit here again soon, and tears would be happy tears next time. Three months later she was right. There we sat, basking in the wonder of human life forming once again. This time was different though. In the period of time between the loss of my first baby and becoming pregnant again, I received a phone call from my best friend. She was pregnant too – due the same time as I was originally due – and she let me know she just found out she was having twins. She was distraught. I was numb. She was scared. I was perplexed. She was anxious. I was so happy for her. I was sad for me.

After that phone call, I went into my bedroom and lay on my bed. Staring at the wallpaper, I cried. Not sobbing or wailing, just gentle soothing tears, and I asked God if I could please have twins one day too. I promised Him that I would never complain about them and that I would always love them and be devoted to raising them to the best of my ability. I had already been to my doctor during the week, and he had run all kinds of tests on me to make sure I was healthy and ready to start trying again to have another baby. He ran every single test on me except a pregnancy test. I found out the next day that I was pregnant again and didn't know it. When my friend called me with her news about two babies, I didn't know I was pregnant. When I cried to God in a prayer to have twins, I didn't realize that I was already pregnant, with twins!

I had an appointment for an early ultrasound the following week to make sure that everything was okay. My local GP had said he was concerned about the blood test reading being so high in something I couldn't even pronounce. I waited and worried over the weekend that something was wrong. I was pregnant, but could I be in danger again of losing my baby? I wasn't sure, so worrying was the easiest thing for me to do. Faith sat there at bay trying to get in. I later learned the power of faith and how to lose the fear in my life. I wouldn't want to go back to my fear life ever again.

Faith rules!

No.

More.

Fear.

I arrived for my ultrasound appointment. My Dad drove me and my Mum came inside with me. My husband was working. He was always busy. The radiologist began to run the scanner over my belly. I don't even know what made me ask (except perhaps that faith was beginning to work in my life), "Is there just one baby in there?" to which she promptly replied, "No. Well actually, there are two healthy heartbeats in there."

She smiled.

I cried.

We all cheered.

TWINS!

My Mum and I walked out of the dimly lit room into the waiting room where my Dad was sitting, reading the newspaper. When we told him he stood up and dropped his paper and magazines, and we all hugged and couldn't believe it. Twins! I was pregnant with twins.

God answered my prayer. I felt like the most special person on Planet Earth.

Our next visit was to the doctor's office. He told me not to rush out and buy a twin stroller as it looked like one of the twins may not make it. I went from elation to deflation in one moment of time. The medical report read, "pending dissolution of the lower conceptus." Twin One's heart beat was racing, and they didn't know if that could be a sign that he wasn't going to make it. During the next nine months, fear and faith both warred for my attention and affection. By the time my boys were born – yes they made it, and yes I made it – I had well and truly learned to have faith in a miracle-working God. During this season I distinctly remember the transition of living with fear as my default mode, to living with faith as my default mode. I couldn't have hoped for better preparation for parenthood.

My husband wasn't overly excited in the beginning. He was still saddened by the loss of our first baby and had become used to the idea of us having no kids. I became pregnant again so quickly he didn't really have time to warm up to the idea, or that's at least what I told myself. I didn't know much of what was going on inside his heart and mind at the time, except that he was deeply concerned that I would be too busy looking after babies and would not be able to provide for his needs, too. That day, we stopped by my husband's work on the way home from the hospital so I could tell him this amazing news in person. I arrived with the ultrasound photos in an envelope. I handed him the envelope so he could open the surprise himself. He was upset and disinterested. He handed back the envelope. I couldn't just leave so I blurted out, "We're having twins!" He was shocked but still upset. I had bothered him and apparently it wasn't his time to celebrate. This was his time of needing to grow up, but again, his choice and not mine.

Please grow up.

Now.

Pregnancy was interesting for me. I found it both cherishing and challenging. I loved every single moment of it. I was sick and tired for much of it and afraid for some of it, but I learned to live by faith for all of it. Visits to my doctor provided me with some solace. He would ask me how I was doing, and I would say I was good but then would burst into tears. Visit after visit I made the most of having someone I could talk to because I knew I couldn't talk to my family or friends. I had supposed that all the anger would stop, and home would become a haven of peace, finally. The anger didn't stop. My plan didn't work. My plan was based on the hope that bringing children into our home would bring peace. It brought such mixed emotions that I can barely describe that season with any accuracy.

Elation, deflation.

Happiness, fury.

Peace, war.

Hope, shattered.

Again.

Time.

Times.

Pretty much all the time.

Pregnancy was no exception. I had hoped it would change everything, but it seemed to have the opposite effect. Everything became harder, more polarized.

I became more afraid.

He became more distant.

We became more strained.

Outbursts of anger.

Strained conversations.

Prolonged silence.

Tears.

Many tears.

One Sunday we were driving somewhere. I think we were driving to church.

Something I said made my husband mad.

Really mad.

He was so mad that I feared what would happen next, so I quickly jumped out of our car and started walking fast in the opposite direction. To my horror, a car stopped by me, and the driver asked me if I was ok. This was so scary for me. Someone saw. Someone noticed. Someone asked me about it. I assured the kind stranger that I was absolutely fine and on my way home. I still however, had to face my husband when I finally arrived home.

I had tried to explain to my doctor that I didn't know what to do as my husband didn't want children. He felt he was too young. He was 26, and we had been married five years. In my awkward pain, I had tried to paint a picture of hope that he someday would accept them. My doctor was kind and said, "Don't worry my dear. When those boys are born, he will love them." Yes! He was right.

When our sons were born, my husband did love them, and he hasn't stopped loving them. Loving them, however, looked different for him than it did for me. For me, loving them meant laying my life down for the next twenty-one years to love and look after them and to raise them to become fine young men. For my husband, loving them was different. For him, it meant loving them without having to do anything for them. He used to remind me – he had trained me – that he loved me but that meant he wasn't required to do anything for me. No flowers, no chocolates, no cards, no faithfulness, no promises. Just love. I got used to that kind of love. However, I wasn't sure how he was planning to raise our children using that kind of love.

I knew that my sons would love their Dad. Their love would be tangible and unconditional and I wanted to do everything I could to help that happen. I wouldn't be the one to shatter their dreams about any aspect of their Dad's life. He loved them and that was enough for me. He loved me and that was enough for me. So we would learn to build a family with a special kind of love. Some would regard it as thoroughly dysfunctional, and others would regard it as stoically strange. Although I was prepared to live with this special kind of love for the rest of my life, I wondered how it would affect our sons in the future.

It was one evening around Christmas. I can recall the time of year vividly as I walked into our home after a rare time out at the movies with some friends. I walked into my home, into what resembled a crime scene. Yet another episode of property destroyed in a fit of rage. The little Christmas tree – a gift from my Grandmother – that I had lovingly assembled for so many years had been kicked from one end of the house to the other. The large antique birdcage given to me by my father had been all but destroyed.

Anger.

Anger ruled.

Again.

I had walked unprepared into all too familiar fall out. I was so upset I finally decided that I would go ahead and actually do something about it this time. I had made that decision countless times for many, many years, but didn't have the courage to follow through.

There were no locks on any doors in our home. Access was always immediate, and there was no place to hide when things got out of hand. That night I was so upset by the scene I had walked in on that I called out for a confrontation. Was I crazy? Yes. Did I care? At that point, no. Where were my kids? Home. When I confronted my husband about his rage, he chased me into the bathroom, and I crouched down, huddled in a ball beside the toilet. I cowered in the corner while he towered over me.

I was afraid.

I was numb.

Motionless.

I knew he wasn't trying to hurt me. He was just trying to help me understand him, but his method always frightened me.

I couldn't hear anything.

I couldn't feel anything.

Deaf.

Numb.

The turning point of my life happened that night in a split second. I looked up and between my husband's legs I could see one of our sons standing in the hallway looking into my eyes through his father's giant stance over me. He was staring with tears rolling down his cheeks, yet even in his fear he made no sound. That was it. That moment changed my life and our lives forever. In that moment in time I realized that I was reproducing my silence in my son. He had somehow learned to not say anything. He knew what he was watching wasn't right but he couldn't do anything about it. I knew if I didn't follow through on getting help that I would successfully reproduce my dysfunction in my sons.

Enough was enough.

A line was drawn in the sand that night.

By me.

7 KEYS TO LIVING IN THE GRACE ZONE

1.   **You can't do it on your own.**
      The amazing thing about living in the grace zone is that you recognize how different it is to living in a war zone.

2.   **You have peace.**
      Peace that transcends all understanding.

3.   **You know everything will work out in the end.**
      Even though you may not be able to see straight right now, you know in your heart that God has a new path for you.

4.   **You have the best interest of everyone at heart.**
      Even if your spouse has hurt you beyond measure, grace allows you to wish the best for him and his future.

5.   **You are careful with your words.**
      The more careful you are with your words, the less regret you will have to deal with in the future.

6.   **You are mindful of your actions.**
      People are watching you and how well you respond in a crisis. Now is the time to exemplify how great grace is.

7.   **You believe you have a future and a hope.**
      There is a quiet confidence and rich assurance that God will make a masterpiece out of your mess.

grace

"Amazing Grace, how sweet the sound,
That saved a wretch like me.
I was once lost but now am found,
Was blind, but now I see."[1]

John Newton [1725-1807]

chapter four

the grace years

grace

grace

grace

Once I drew that line in the sand, I had to stay on the safe side of it. I called my church and asked to speak to a woman counselor who I had heard had a reputation for being very pro-marriage. After all, I was looking for someone to help me stay married, not for someone who would tell me to walk away. I was so afraid of meeting her – afraid that she would judge me somehow for not being able just to stay married and get on with it. I had tried – and I wanted her to know how hard I was trying.

I brought a notebook and pen with me to the meeting, sitting on my lap like a security blanket. When I explained a little of my story (knowing full well that there are always two sides and that my husband would always be forthcoming with his side of the story), I asked right away if she could please help me with some keys to success. Perhaps she could give me a list of things I could improve to make my marriage work. Maybe I had missed something big that I was about to find out about. I was willing. I was always very willing to try.

I held my breath as she took her time to respond to my high anxiety. I will never forget the feeling that flooded my life – past, present and future – when she finally replied. "My dear, you can put the notebook down now." I felt numb. Again. Putting the notebook down would signify putting the security blanket aside. That would mean vulnerability. That would mean permission to be in pain. That would mean I am falling apart and don't need to pretend by sticking myself back together.

Permission to cry.

Permission to breathe.

Finally.

Permission to break the silence.

My counselor handed me a book called "Love Must Be Tough" by Dr. James Dobson. I had never heard of him before, and I didn't know what tough love was. She asked me to read the book and do what it said, and after I had done those two things she would see me again. I did what she asked and made an appointment to meet with my husband.

The fact that I needed to make an appointment with him was all too telling of that season in our lives. I still loved him dearly. He still loved me dearly – I knew he did – but we couldn't keep living like this. It was highly organized dysfunction at its peak. A friend took the boys to the park so that we could be alone at home for my meeting. We sat down, and I explained to my husband how very much I loved him. I was already crying and hardly able to speak. He sat there looking at me, probably wondering what was wrong with me this time. I summoned the courage to let him know that he would need to leave and then come back so we could start again as a family. I explained that we couldn't keep going on like this and that I was afraid for our sons and what would happen to them in the midst of all the crazy craziness.

He was deeply shocked but still somewhat detached. He too had learned to live numb. We both cried. He didn't have anywhere to go (which is why I didn't ever want to ask him to leave because I knew he wouldn't know what to do or where to go). I had become like a mother figure or big sister figure in his life where I spent all my time and energy looking after him, making sure he had everything he needed. I loved to do that. I just never expected anything in return, because that would only lead to more disappointment.

He left and didn't come back home.

Gone.

My husband found a place to stay – he moved in with a girlfriend of his who willingly obliged to assume the role of looking after him. That wasn't what I had hoped for; it wasn't what I had faith for. It wasn't the way the book said it could work out. I figured that he would leave and come back with flowers and chocolates and an apology that matched the size of our lives together thus far. I got nothing.

He was remorseful.

He was always regretful.

Remorse and regret without the will to change.

I was left empty and alone. I had caused this to happen because I spoke up. It was my fault, but I knew not to chase him back. He would come back right away, but it would be business as usual. He reminded me that he was only able to be who he was – nothing more, nothing less. Any extra expectations I could possibly have towards him changing would only end up in more frustration and further disappointment.

So I learned to trust God again at a whole new level.

Trust God.

Trust.

God.

Time passes and wounds heal when treated properly. In spite of the pain caused by my separation from my husband, for the first time in a long time I was able to experience the wonder of the miracle-working power of God in healing my broken heart and life. This was, above all else, the best gift I could ever give my children – a healthy me.

The process of becoming a healthy me was one that could not be forced. Time takes us along at a non-negotiable pace sometimes, and the pace of healing falls into that category. I still loved my former husband, and the love was so well worn that I knew it wouldn't ever go away. But I came to love him like my brother. The fire of romance smoldered and burnt out. Any hope that we would be back together as a happy couple had flown far, far away. In this period of great grace, I had to learn what it was to love and let go. I don't mean that I learned to let go of love but that I learned to let go of a life that could no longer be part of me. I would often go back in time wondering what went so wrong, and what more I could have done to fix it, but the time finally came when I knew what we had couldn't be resurrected.

That was when I decided to make the very final decision to get a divorce. It wasn't what I had wanted or hoped for, but I could no longer ignore the fact that my marriage was beyond repair. Each day presented me with the ever-more demanding choice: would I choose a past I once dreamed of, or would I choose a future unknown? Faith compelled me forward.

Some people are very quick to remind people like me that God hates divorce. Yes, He does, and so do I. In fact I think I would be hard pressed to find a single soul who has been through a divorce who actually enjoyed the process. It is just not possible. God does hate divorce. He also hates abuse, adultery, idolatry, gossip, and all kinds of other sins – great and small. I, for one, do not care to sit in judgment over people's relationships whether they are working well or not. God knows all, sees all, and loves all. My role is to trust God and leave the judging to His infinite knowledge, wisdom and greatest capacity to love.

I sat in the courtroom on that fateful day of my divorce afraid, very afraid. I was trying my best to exercise faith so that fear would dissipate. I said over and over in my mind, "Don't worry about anything, pray about everything." I couldn't remember the exact words from the Bible, but I knew what I needed. I knew I needed to not worry, and I knew I needed to pray. Then my name was called. I stood to my feet and the Judge asked me, "Do you want this divorce? Answer yes or no. Do you want this divorce?" Everything inside me wanted to scream, "NO! I DO NOT WANT THIS DIVORCE! Can you please rephrase this question, your Honor!"

I composed myself, something that I had long learned how to do in public, and I replied, "Yes, your Honor, I want this divorce."

I lied.

I cried.

peace

"Be anxious for nothing, but in everything by prayer and supplication, with thanksgiving, let your requests be made known to God; and the peace of God, which surpasses all understanding, will guard your hearts and minds through Christ Jesus."

philippians chapter four verses six and seven
[new king james version]

I didn't want this divorce.

I needed this divorce.

We don't always want what we need.

I believe that what I did at the time was the right thing. I made that decision for myself, and my children. It was by far the hardest decision I have ever had to make, and I would never want to make it again. Once is enough for anyone.

This is what I remember as being a great grace period of my life - the fact that I had the courage to have the conversation that would bring about such drastic change was a true miracle.

The fact that now people would know about us was something I had to learn to live with. I had learned to live my silent years like a pro. I now had to learn to live my public years with great grace. People would look and stare. Some would judge, and others would console. I didn't care to talk about it in the midst of my crazy years, and I certainly didn't want to start talking about it later. Details are always delicious morsels to people who lack excitement in their lives. I, however, had had enough excitement in my life to hold my hand over my mouth forever. Those who have lived in similar situations as mine have their own details to recall and relate to, and those who don't have any idea what it is like don't actually need details of the drama.

There is still a silent mystery surrounding that season of my life that will stay unspoken this side of Eternity. For the sake of my children and the sake of my former husband and his family no further details need to be shared.

I have no desire to cast a shadow on another living soul.

Don't worry about anything.

Pray about everything.

Don't worry.

Pray.

My children have always had their Dad in their lives, and they love him dearly and he loves them dearly. I am grateful for their lifelong love for each other. I wouldn't want anything less because anything less would mean loss for each of them. So I have learned to manage and deal with personal pain and disappointment that comes from seasons of my sons' lives where Dad was a hero, but not behaving heroically. I had to learn how to build my life. I had learned how to survive, but now I knew my children needed us to thrive. I took the challenge to move from surviving to thriving head on, and I took it seriously. That decision landed me in the last place I would have expected to find a home for people as messed up as I was – church.

It was there, at church, that I met The Word (the Word Who became flesh and moved into my neighborhood).

It took time for the numbness of my decision to divorce and build a new life to wear into reality. I had embraced most of my moving on season but there was still an area of my life that I had kept closed, the idea that I would ever fall in love again.

Man of God enters the room of my life.

The room of my heart.

Man of God.

My heart.

Peace.

7 KEYS TO BLISSFUL BABY YEARS

1. **Be thankful.**
    You may be overwhelmed right now, but always be thankful for the little life you brought into the world and remember the privilege it is to be a parent.

2. **Sleep when you can.**
    Sleep deprivation is a form of torture, and when you aren't sleeping you quite possibly aren't thinking clearly. Sleep when you can and remember this season will pass.

3. **Focus on the future.**
    Every day, remember you and your kids have a purpose. When hard times come, focus on the future.

4. **Enjoy this season.**
    In a flash, it will be over, so enjoy the good times and do your best to minimize the drama times.

5. **Ask for help.**
    Ask your parents for help or ask your friends for help if you need it. Don't be ashamed and don't be an island. Reach out if you feel like you aren't coping.

6. **Stay healthy.**
    Remember to eat well and exercise when you can. You will feel better when you look after yourself, body and soul.

7. **Read regularly.**
    Read your Bible and read any great parenting books that could help you handle this season well.

    Remember, our personal decisions have generational implications.

choices

"Well married a person has wings, poorly married shackles."[1]

Henry Ward Beecher

chapter five

the forever years

forever

forever

forever

Now that I was on my own with my boys I had certain freedoms that I didn't have before, like not only attending church, but now being involved at church. I loved to volunteer, and I had administrative skills, meaning I could volunteer from my home or the office and having the boys with me was never a problem. We learned to serve together. I loved God and wanted to serve Him ever since I was a little girl. I didn't know what that looked like for us now, but I did get on with serving in any way I could. I loved our church and enjoyed learning more and more about God and His Word – so much so that I decided to enroll in Bible College for a year, so that my head could catch up with my heart. I read my Bible over the years, but only in bits and pieces, mainly the Gospels and Psalms. But the desire was growing inside of me -- I wanted and needed to understand more of it. Enrolling in Bible College was one of the best decisions of my life, and it was there that I got to know my husband Jonathan William Wilson, who was a pastor at my church.

It was a very different experience for me – getting to know a Godly man who loved Jesus more than me. As interested as I was in getting to know Jonathan, I was also very aware of the life I had come from and the fact that I didn't want to ever get married again. I just wanted to be safe and without perpetual pain. That was my goal. So when Jonathan started to court my friendship I was very wary of him and even of my own heart. I could not work out what he saw in me and I could not work out how he could be as lovely and wonderful as he was. I feared it would all stop at some unsuspecting time in our future.

I was suspicious and still hurting.

My mental map of men – based on my life experiences so far – was about to be blown up.

I trusted God, but I wasn't about to trust another man in my life anytime soon. What's more, I wasn't about to introduce anyone into my sons' lives that could possibly cause them any more grief than what we had just departed from.

Much responsibility rested on my shoulders.

Way too much.

Trust takes years to build and an instant to break. I was now in a new building phase of my life, so this automatically included trust in the package. I had learned to trust God but now I knew I had to learn to trust man, or rather in this instance, a man of God. I did everything possible to shoo him away including continually stating the fact that I was not looking for a relationship and that me and my boys were all good. We would be fine on our own. It seemed that the more independent I showed myself to be, the more interested he became. He figured that I must have had my life somehow worked out to not be a needy woman. He had been through his own private pain. He had fought long and hard for his first marriage to work, and he was not looking for a new partner simply for the sake of not being alone.

By the time we met and started to get to know each other, we had already been through so much pain and so many refining fires. We were readier than I cared to recognize at the time to make a commitment to being together for the rest of our lives. I knew that I would never feel ready to get married again. I had done that once, and that once was supposed to be forever. Perhaps I could bypass all the fuss of a wedding and just say "I do" under a tree with an old sentimental handkerchief, like the scene in "Braveheart." That would be perfect. I wanted to avoid all fuss, and I wanted to avoid all focus on me. I was still healing but not yet healed. The good news is that Jonathan knew where I was at, and he was prepared to commit to me and commit to my healing process. He saw my willingness to continue on the healing and wholeness road. He loved me, and he was more than happy to show me, tell me, bless me, carry me. I had never known love like this before. He was so active in his love for me that I didn't at times know quite how to respond.

He had fallen in love with me before we had even had our first date. He vowed not to take any woman out for even a coffee unless he knew that she would be his future wife. He had a level of sensitivity and maturity and trust in God that I had never seen before. I often think about how risky it was for him to fall in love with me, but he assures me, even to this day, that there was no risk. He knew. God helped him know. I wanted to know God like that. Jonathan has helped me know God like that. That confident assurance that God is with us in our decision-making has made all the world of difference in my life.

Our first date was a little unconventional. It included fifty of the most incredibly beautiful field roses I have ever seen, dinner at one of the most romantic restaurants I have ever been to, diamond earrings as a little token gift of friendship, and an evening at the theatre with box seats to "Beauty and the Beast." If this evening was not enough I was picked up again the next morning for another day of bliss with this amazing man who just lived to love. His love was a doing kind of love, an active kind of love.

A kind of love without restraint.

Apparently without bounds.

A love that required no reason.

To love.

To give.

To share.

Bless.

I hadn't ever known a love like this before. Our next date – the very next day – we lunched at a beautiful sunny Sydney café followed by a visit to the store I had never been to before called Tiffany & Co. It was such a fun date!

I loved to play dress-up as a kid, and I was like a kid in a dress-up store with all the beautiful diamonds and jewels. Jonathan was so much fun! He asked the sales assistant to show me many rings, and then he pointed out one in particular and asked her to hand it to me. I looked at it, staring deeply into its rarity, its flawless quality, its unique beauty. Jonathan reached towards the ring, taking it gently from me – not in a rugged way that would cause me to shut down and stop dreaming. He took my left hand and gently, slowly and very intentionally placed that ring on my finger. It was the biggest diamond I had ever seen in real life. It was magnificent, unlike me. I took the ring off and said something to the effect of, "Well that was fun – what are we going to do now?" I was just about as uncomfortable as I could possibly be. Awkward officially. What was happening? Was he about to propose? Was he seriously thinking about buying such a beautiful ring for such a poor wretch like me?

We left the store, and I left that dream behind. We were going on to some other adventure for the day and back to normal life. Some weeks passed, and we were due to fly out to Africa for a missions trip that I had saved up for and prayed for, for years. There were seven of us on that trip and Jonathan was the leader. It was dawn on my twenty-ninth birthday at Busua Beach in Ghana, West Africa, and Jonathan had asked me to come for a walk along the beach. I knew that he was up to something but I didn't know what. All of a sudden he held my hand tightly and stopped me in my tracks. He looked into my eyes and he embraced my soul. He paused for a brief moment before lowering himself slowly onto one knee.

He proposed.

I accepted.

What had I done? Fortunately, all the excitement of the thought of a brand new, wonder life had taken up most of my available worrying space. I recall that season as being one of sheer joy, with an overwhelming sense of the goodness and faithfulness of God in my life. Jonathan loved my sons. That was something that I thought could be a problem between us, but it never has been. His capacity to love is breathtaking.

It wasn't until we arrived home that the reality of my decision set in. My family was, and still is very happy for us, and my boys loved Jonathan and his beautiful twelve-year-old daughter, Rachel. The two older children that Jonathan raised from his first marriage had grown up and left home. Jonathan's first-born son Joshua lived in specialized care in a home for the severely handicapped. Joshua was born with the umbilical cord around his neck and so tragically, became brain damaged at birth. He has improved a little over his lifetime but not a lot. He is unable to communicate or care for himself. He is a wonderful young man who lives in his own world, his own permanent now. He is a happy soul who will one day dance in Heaven. So here we were, his, hers and the thought of potentially ours to come.

When Jonathan proposed to me in Africa, he placed a beautiful shell on my finger and told me that he would replace it with my ring when we arrived home. I assured him that I didn't need a fancy ring and that this little shell was all the love I could ever want on my finger. However, he was a man on a mission, determined to show and prove evidence of his love for me. He planned another date day to take me to Tiffany & Co. again. The first time I was loving living the dream, but this time reality had set in, and I knew that there was no way he could buy that ring for me. We found the same sales assistant and he selected the same ring, and he placed it gently and very intentionally on my finger. I remained composed and pleasant, but felt hopelessly awkward. I thanked all involved and asked if we could leave now. We moved on to have lunch and a conversation about being realistic! I deeply appreciated that he would even think to take me to a store like that, let alone consider buying me anything from there. I wanted however to move on and find something that we both loved and that would be a more perfect fit.

We came across an estate store that had cases and cases of pre-loved estate jewelry. I looked and looked until I found something that somewhat resembled the Tiffany & Co. ring. It was a large diamond, and it was a fraction of the cost. Perfect. The sales assistant offered us champagne and a discount, something that Tiffany & Co. had not. I didn't want champagne, but that discount sounded good. What I needed most was fresh air, so I stepped outside. It was the bright light outside that helped me make my decision. The sales assistant encouraged me to hold it up in the light so I could really see it, and that's what I did. I held this diamond ring up to the light, and this is what I saw: it was wide, but it had no depth. It was a clear in color but flawed in quality. There were black speckles all throughout this large shallow stone. No wonder it was significantly lower in price.

I was ready to leave.

I needed to breathe.

We jumped in the car and silence filled the air. I couldn't talk because I had too much to say. I wanted to say so much to Jonathan along the lines of him being able to do much better than settling for a girl like me. I wanted to tell him that I was happy to settle with the cheap ring but I couldn't make that story sound real. I wanted to tell him that the time with him in Tiffany & Co. trying on all of the princess rings made me feel more special as a woman than I had ever felt. And it wasn't about the price tags. It was way deeper than that. All of these conflicting conversations were going on in my head simultaneously.

Meanwhile, I hadn't even noticed that we were on the road again, heading back towards Tiffany & Co. Now I felt traumatized. What were we doing? I didn't know what we were doing, but I knew that he knew what he was doing. Trust. There's that word again. We walked back inside and found the same sales assistant. This would be our third and final visit around this subject. Jonathan took me by the hand and walked me confidently over to the counter. He didn't need to say a word as the sales assistant brought the ring out of the showcase and handed it to him. This time he took my hand more firmly, somehow knowing that he needed to arrest and calm the anxiety inside me. He placed the ring on my finger this time with such intention that I didn't know if I could ever take it off. The sales assistant placed a mirror in front of me and encouraged me to take a look in the light.

I took a deep breath and looked deeply into the mirror, which appeared to me to be like a mirror of truth. Tears streamed down my face as I realized what was happening. This wasn't about wealth. This was about worth. Jonathan told me that he had always only ever wanted this ring for me but had allowed me to come to that conclusion for myself. He didn't force his love on me. He allowed me time to process and see for myself that I didn't have to keep believing that I was broken goods, good for a secondhand life with a secondhand ring. The Holy Spirit spoke to me so clearly in that instant about my worth, and I have never been the same again.

My worth.

Never the same again.

We were engaged for six months and then on April 5th, 1997 we married. I walked down that aisle still somewhat afraid. I wasn't concerned that Jonathan wasn't right for me, nor good enough for me. I was concerned that I wasn't right for him, nor good enough for him. I had many conversations with him prior to our big day, encouraging him to feel free to seek out better suitors, perhaps women who were more ministry material. I didn't see myself as a Pastor's wife, let alone a Pastor. Ever. I felt as though he deserved better than me and all I had to offer. I loved God with all of my heart, and I loved people. He said he knew what he was doing, so I learned to trust his lead. He was right, and yes, we are perfect together. Perfect in all of our wonderful human imperfection. We married on purpose for His purpose. He, a man of God with the attributes of a saint. Me, a woman of God with the potential for improvement. We have enjoyed many years together now, and yes, he is still a saint, and yes, I still have room for improvement.

Our common bond is purpose. We believe that we have been created by God on purpose for His purpose. And although we both went through so much pain in our first marriages, we know that everything that happens is either God sent or God used, and there is no wastage in Him. God did not send pain our way, but he did send promise, potential and a plan for our future together.

Our future together.

Ours.

Together.

Forever.

Jonathan William Wilson is my Boaz.

You will need to read the story – the entire book of Ruth in the Bible – to know the kind of man that Boaz was.

Redeemer.

masterpiece

"Meanwhile, the moment we get tired in the waiting, God's Spirit is right alongside helping us along. If we don't know how or what to pray, it doesn't matter. He does our praying in and for us, making prayer out of our wordless sighs, our aching groans. He knows us far better than we know ourselves, knows our pregnant condition, and keeps us present before God. That's why we can be so sure that every detail in our lives of love for God is worked into something good."

romans chapter eight verses twenty-six to twenty-eight
[the message]

7 KEYS TO HAPPILY EVER AFTER

1. **Leave your past in the past.**
    Do your best to focus on the future and don't bring the damage from your past relationship into your new relationship.

2. **Don't draw comparisons.**
    The person you are now with is not your ex. Be careful not to draw comparisons, just as you appreciate those comparisons not being drawn about you.

3. **Go on dates.**
    Make a point to go on a weekly date for lunch or dinner or just out for a coffee. That should be your time together to focus on each other without distractions.

4. **Be respectful.**
    Choose your words, your tone of voice and your timing, carefully and lovingly.

5. **Never use the "D" word.**
    We frame our world with our words. Divorce should be deleted from your vocabulary.

6. **Forgive quickly.**
    The quicker you forgive, the sooner you get to start again.

7. **Choose to love.**
    Love is a doing word. When you don't 'feel' like being loving, that is the time that you should choose to love anyway.

perspective

"A person isn't who they are during the last conversation you had with them – they're who they've been throughout your whole relationship."[1]

Rainer Maria Rilke

part two

boys guys men

defined

BOY

A male child, from birth to full growth, especially one less than 18 years of age. A young man who lacks maturity, judgment, etc.

GUY

A man; a fellow. Informal persons of either sex.

MAN

An adult male person, as distinguished from a boy or a woman.

Is there really a difference between a boy, a guy, and a man? Here's what the dictionary says. A boy is a male child from birth to full growth, especially one less than 18 years of age. That's a boy. Finding a cute boy and thinking that he's adorable might be fun, but he is not a man. He is a boy. We do not want to marry a boy until the boy has become a man. What is a guy? Even a cute guy? A guy is an informal term for persons of either sex. Who wants to marry that? We need to stop and ask ourselves, was I not born for more than this? For more than a nice boy or a cute guy?

I have one husband, three sons and three daughters. I have given birth to boys, and my goal has always been to raise them from boyhood to manhood. I have given birth to girls, and my goal has always been to raise them from girlhood to womanhood. There is nothing wrong with guys (informal persons of either sex), but I wouldn't want to see my children settle for a life's partner who merely lives a "guy" life.

Some guys are nice guys, and some are not very nice at all.

One evening I was taking a stroll down the boardwalk in Santa Monica with a group of friends who were visiting from Australia. There were around thirty of us altogether, and we walked in small clusters so as not to take up all the space. I was walking close to a friend and her husband while my husband Jonathan was a distance behind with some of our other friends. As we walked and talked and enjoyed the evening breeze I noticed three people walking towards us, so I moved aside a little closer to my friend so they could pass.

The three people were tall, nice looking, Europeans (I think). There were two young men and one young woman. As we passed each other, one of the young men gently bumped into me and as he did so, he reached his hand into my blouse and groped me.

He then quickly slipped his hand out and continued walking with his friends as though nothing had happened. I was so shocked I felt numb with the vivid recollection of what just took place. I kept walking for a few paces as though nothing had happened, and my friend kept talking to me because she didn't see anything.

All of a sudden I stopped and said to my friend and her husband, "Oh my gosh! Did you see what that guy just did?" They hadn't seen anything except the three of them walk by closely. At that moment, something came over me and I turned around and I shouted, "That guy! That guy just groped me!" The young woman glanced over her shoulder but the three of them kept walking.

I was justifiably upset and mad at being violated in this way.

I knew what this guy had done, and he knew what he had done, and he obviously thought he could get away with it. My shouts became louder, "That guy! Stop him! That guy just groped me!" Just as I finally caught the attention of a group of our friends who were lingering back, they called out to me, "What? What!" The distance between where I was standing, and my group of friends behind was around fifty feet, so the long distance shouting caught the attention of everyone on the boardwalk. I wanted to run away. I was so embarrassed. These three were just about to push right through the middle of my friends, thinking they were a group of strangers. Two of my very tall man friends grabbed this guy and spun him around. He gestured that he didn't know what they were talking about, and I motioned that he did what he did. That made me even more determined to make sure he didn't get away with it. He did it to me, and he was sure to do it again. It was his special "move," no doubt.

The guy tried to get out of it and wriggle away; but my men friends held their ground. I could not believe this was happening. They had him by both arms and began to walk him over towards me. I freaked out and said, "No! No! I don't want to talk to him! I don't want him anywhere near me!" My men friends wanted him to apologize, but by this point I had broken down and I just wanted to go home. I called out to them to let him go. I certainly didn't want another close-up encounter with him. We went back to the hotel where we were staying, and I was deeply embarrassed by the whole incident. My husband was at least one hundred feet behind me so hadn't seen or heard anything. When he finally caught up with my men friends, and then with me, he was outraged. I am so grateful that Jonathan didn't see it happen otherwise there would have been a brawl at the beach!

I was beside myself that night. Embarrassed and inexplicably ashamed of what happened. I was upset about what this guy did to me, and I was equally upset about speaking up about it. No wonder most women don't say anything. I knew however I had to say something. I knew that this guy had done this before and that he would do it again. He was a smooth operator and got the shock of his life when he walked into a pack of men who consider themselves their sister's keeper

That night highlighted the difference between guys and men. This guy's friends did nothing to stop him or help me. And my men friends did everything they possibly could to stop and scare the daylights out of him. They didn't hurt him physically although they may have wanted to. They gave him a stern warning that they would be watching him, and they did. My men friends told me the next morning that some of them had gone back out for a late night drive to see if they could track him, but they didn't find him. Thank goodness!

This man was young, tall, good looking and didn't appear at all to be a creeper who would do such a thing. It just shows that you can't judge a book by its cover, especially when it comes to the opposite sex.

Let's talk about a man, shall we? A man is an adult male person, an adult, as distinguished from a boy, or a woman. A "boy", or a "guy" was never intended by God or can never replace the role of a "man" in our lives.

God does not choose our mate for us, but He does give us very clear direction in His Word on how to choose our mate. We get that lovely, joyous task of choosing that mate for ourselves, which means that when we step foot down the aisle, the "I do" aisle, there is an element of risk involved.

However spiritual, perceptive or insightful we are, nobody knows exactly how things are going to work out in the end. Even if we were perfect, which we aren't, we are marrying somebody who is also imperfect, and we don't know anything perfectly!

So that walk down the "I do" aisle always has an element of risk and uncertainty to it. We must navigate through this uncertainty with our eyes open, but we also need to be women who believe God, trust God and learn to trust the person we're saying "I do" to. Somehow we've got to try to make it all work. That is not always as easy and straightforward as we would like it to be.

God may have certain people in His mind for us, but ultimately we are the ones who make the decision. We are the ones who choose our partner.

Choose wisely!

attention

"It took a long time, but I've finally figured it out. When it comes to men who are romantically interested in you, it's really simple. Just ignore everything they say and only pay attention to what they do."[1]

The Last Lecture
by Randy Pausch

manners

My man loves me this I know,
For his manners tell me so.
When he opens up the door,
It just makes me love him more.

Yes, oh he loves me!
Yes, oh he loves me!
Yes, oh he loves me!
His manners tell me so!

My man loves me yes indeed,
For he offers me his seat.
Leads the way for me to say,
That is why he's mine OK!

Yes, oh he loves me!
Yes, oh he loves me!
Yes, oh he loves me!
His manners tell me so!

Manners Maketh a Man.

I am very grateful to be married to a man with impeccable manners. I am very grateful to be married to a man of character who chooses not to compromise his values; our values. I am beyond grateful to be married to a man whose role model is Jesus. And he is grateful to be married to a woman who doesn't get her "J's" mixed up. Jesus is my Lord and Savior. Jonathan is my husband. I already have a Lord and Savior, and therefore don't require my husband to be my Lord or my Savior. He is very relieved about that!

Jonathan is human.

All men are.

All women are too.

Our humanity has an opportunity to be formed and forged into the character of the greatest Man that ever lived. God chose to send His Son Jesus to earth as a fully human man and still fully God.

Whether we are a man or a woman, Jesus is our best example. When I think about Jesus, I do think about what an awesome MAN he was. God – yes! But God and MAN. His LIFE on earth has given a road map for us to live by.

Who is this MAN?

What was His MANNER?

Manners are not just remembering to say "please" and "thank you," opening a car door, or standing for a lady, although all of those things (and more) are very appreciated. Manners are the way in which we conduct ourselves, in word and in deed.

Let's look at this amazing MAN:

1.   What does He see?
2.   What does He say?
3.   What would Jesus do?

The closer we follow His example, the more incredible our relationships will become.

Jesus

"Out of the stump of David's family will grow a shoot – yes, a new Branch bearing fruit from the old root. And the Spirit of the LORD will rest on him – the Spirit of wisdom and understanding, the Spirit of counsel and might, the Spirit of knowledge and the fear of the LORD. He will delight in obeying the LORD. He will never judge by appearance, false evidence, or hearsay. He will defend the poor and the exploited. He will rule against the wicked and destroy them with the breath of his mouth. He will be clothed with fairness and truth."

isaiah chapter eleven verses one to five
[new living translation]

1.   What does Jesus see?

The story of the Samaritan woman at the well exemplifies how Jesus – "The Man" treated women who had been mistreated by the world. Jesus neither ignored nor judged her. He also didn't take advantage of her neediness! Jesus saw what LIFE had done to this woman, and He chose to place value on her instead of more pain.

> Soon a Samaritan woman came to draw water, and Jesus said to her, "Please give me a drink." He was alone at the time because his disciples had gone into the village to buy some food. The woman was surprised, for Jews refuse to have anything to do with Samaritans. She said to Jesus, "You are a Jew, and I am a Samaritan woman. Why are you asking me for a drink?" Jesus replied, "If you only knew the gift God has for you and who you are speaking to, you would ask me, and I would give you living water." "But sir, you don't have a rope or a bucket," she said, "and this well is very deep. Where would you get this living water? And besides, do you think you're greater than our ancestor Jacob, who gave us this well? How can you offer better water than he and his sons and his animals enjoyed?" Jesus replied, "Anyone who drinks this water will soon become thirsty again. But those who drink the water I give will never be thirsty again. It becomes a fresh, bubbling spring within them, giving them eternal life." "Please, sir," the woman said, "give me this water! Then I'll never be thirsty again, and I won't have to come here to get water." "Go and get your husband," Jesus told her. "I don't have a husband," the woman replied. Jesus said, "You're right! You don't have a husband – for you have had five husbands, and you aren't even married

to the man you're living with now. You certainly spoke the truth!" "Sir," the woman said, "you must be a prophet. So tell me, why is it that you Jews insist that Jerusalem is the only place of worship, while we Samaritans claim it is here at Mount Gerizim, where our ancestors worshiped?" Jesus replied, "Believe me, dear woman, the time is coming when it will no longer matter whether you worship the Father on this mountain or in Jerusalem. You Samaritans know very little about the one you worship, while we Jews know all about him, for salvation comes through the Jews. But the time is coming—indeed it's here now—when true worshipers will worship the Father in spirit and in truth. The Father is looking for those who will worship him that way. For God is Spirit, so those who worship him must worship in spirit and in truth." The woman said, "I know the Messiah is coming—the one who is called Christ. When he comes, he will explain everything to us." Then Jesus told her, "I am the Messiah!" Just then his disciples came back. They were shocked to find him talking to a woman, but none of them had the nerve to ask, "What do you want with her?" or "Why are you talking to her?" The woman left her water jar beside the well and ran back to the village, telling everyone, "Come and see a man who told me everything I ever did! Could he possibly be the Messiah?" So the people came streaming from the village to see Him."

john chapter four verses seven to thirty
[new living translation]

2.   What does Jesus say?

The Bible says in Ephesians chapter five, verse twenty-five, "Husbands, love your wives." It then goes on to say in verse twenty-eight, "even so, husbands should love their wives."

> "And further, submit to one another out of reverence for Christ. For wives, this means submit to your husbands as to the Lord. For a husband is the head of his wife as Christ is the head of the church. He is the Savior of his body, the church. As the church submits to Christ, so you wives should submit to your husbands in everything. For husbands, this means love your wives, just as Christ loved the church. He gave up his life for her to make her holy and clean, washed by the cleansing of God's word. He did this to present her to himself as a glorious church without a spot or wrinkle or any other blemish. Instead, she will be holy and without fault. In the same way, husbands ought to love their wives as they love their own bodies. For a man who loves his wife actually shows love for himself. No one hates his own body but feeds and cares for it, just as Christ cares for the church. And we are members of his body. As the Scriptures say, "A man leaves his father and mother and is joined to his wife, and the two are united into one." This is a great mystery, but it is an illustration of the way Christ and the church are one. So again I say, each man must love his wife as he loves himself, and the wife must respect her husband.
>
> ephesians chapter five verses twenty-one to thirty-three
> [new living translation]

We should spend our energy loving and serving each other, rather than arguing and throwing Bible verses at each other when we feel disrespected. The Bible says that women should submit to their husband. This is a perfect cue not to rush into marriage with someone you don't trust. Your husband's role is to lead you. Can you let him lead you?

The Bible says that husbands should love their wives "even so." That means that when we, as wives, are being unlovable, God requires our husbands to love, love, love us anyway. That is a magnificent picture of the love of God in sending His Son Jesus to earth to save us. It was the ultimate act of LOVE, LOVE, LOVE for the unlovable.

Remember, the man is the head of the house, but as Toula's mother said in the movie, My Big Fat Greek Wedding, "The woman is the neck that turns the head!"

Let Jesus lead you.

Let Jesus love you.

Let your husband lead you.

Let your husband love you.

3.   What would Jesus do?

"Love endures long and is patient and kind; love never is envious nor boils over with jealousy, is not boastful or vainglorious, does not display itself haughtily. It is not conceited (arrogant and inflated with pride); it is not rude (unmannerly) and does not act unbecomingly. Love (God's love in us) does not insist on its own rights or its own way, for it is not self-seeking; it is not touchy or fretful or resentful; it takes no account of the evil done to it [it pays no attention to a suffered wrong]. It does not rejoice at injustice and unrighteousness, but rejoices when right and truth prevail. Love bears up under anything and everything that comes, is ever ready to believe the best of every person, its hopes are fadeless under all circumstances, and it endures everything [without weakening]. Love never fails [never fades out or becomes obsolete or comes to an end]…"

one corinthians chapter thirteen verses four to eight
[amplified version]

What Would Jesus Do?

1.   Jesus would be patient and kind.

       LOVE endures long and is patient and kind.

       Impatience is a turn off.

2.   Jesus would never be envious or jealous.

       LOVE is never envious or jealous.

       Jealousy is a turn off.

3.   Jesus would not be arrogant or proud.

       LOVE is not arrogant or proud.

       Arrogance and pride is a turn off.

4.   Jesus would not be rude or unmannerly

       LOVE is not rude or unmannerly.

       Rudeness is a turn off.

5.   Jesus would not insist on having His own way.

       LOVE does not insist on having its own way.

       Selfishness is a turn off.

6.   Jesus would not be touchy or resentful.

       LOVE is not touchy or resentful.

       Moodiness and resentfulness is a turn off.

7.   Jesus would keep no account of the evil done to Him.

       LOVE keeps no account of the evil done to it.

       Offense is a turn off.

8.   Jesus would not rejoice at injustice and unrighteousness.

LOVE does not rejoice at injustice and unrighteousness.

Compromise is a turn off.

9.   Jesus would bear up under anything and everything that came His way.

LOVE bears up under anything and everything that comes.

Abdication is a turn off.

10.   Jesus would be ever ready to believe the best of every person.

LOVE is ever ready to believe the best of every person.

Mistrust is a turn off.

WHAT WOMEN REALLY WANT:

- patience
- kindness
- trust
- security
- manners
- selflessness
- stability
- forgiveness
- truth
- faithfulness
- loyalty
- romance and shoes!!

LOVE NEVER FAILS!

reality

"It's so much easier to tell people what they want to hear instead of what they need to hear."[2]

Dr. Phil McGraw

chapter six

ten types of relationships that won't work
caution
beware
danger

bookends

"Love endures long and is patient and kind; love never is envious nor boils over with jealousy, is not boastful or vainglorious, does not display itself haughtily. It is not conceited (arrogant and inflated with pride); it is not rude (unmannerly) and does not act unbecomingly. Love (God's love in us) does not insist on its own rights or its own way, for it is not self-seeking; it is not touchy or fretful or resentful; it takes no account of the evil done to it [it pays no attention to a suffered wrong]. It does not rejoice at injustice and unrighteousness, but rejoices when right and truth prevail. Love bears up under anything and everything that comes, is ever ready to believe the best of every person, its hopes are fadeless under all circumstances, and it endures everything [without weakening]. Love never fails [never fades out or becomes obsolete or comes to an end]."

one corinthians chapter thirteen verses four to eight
[amplified]

Love is the bookends of our life.

Love.

Bookends.

1 Corinthians 13, verses 4-8 is a famous passage of scripture. It's often written in cards from one lover to another. It is often read out at weddings as the scripture to mark the special "I do" day. It is often referred to in romantic terms about what love is.

When you meet the man of your dreams, that amazing man that is going to be your partner for life, love is at the beginning. Love is the first bookend. Seeing all of these things in your relationship, knowing that he is beautiful and kind, and patient and loving, that is the beginning of our relationship. This is the first bookend in our life – it is right, it is good. It is not just an ideal. It is what God wants in our marriages, and as Christians, it is right. We absolutely should seek these things in our partners.

The second bookend is also love.

This love is about Eternity.

We start our marriage with love. We're meant to end our marriage, till death do us part, with love being the other bookend. At the end of our lives together, our love should be just like it was the day we said, "I do", but even more intensely passionate. That is what is supposed to happen, the ideal. So what do we do about all the years in between, if this is lacking or absent? Stop and think about it. What do we do when anything thing tries to exalt itself above love in our relationship? What do we do when impatience creeps in on the honeymoon? What do we do when unmannerly rudeness happens in the first five months of marriage? What do we do when there's conflict or disappointment of any kind in our relationship? It will undoubtedly happen in some way, shape or form. For the entire span of our marriages, we will have to continually give our all so that love will always prevail and pull rank on anything that tries to exalt itself above it.

If we don't start with love, we have no hope.

If we don't end with love, we have no hope.

If you are not yet married, we are going to look at ten kinds of relationships that don't work. If I can help rescue one person from going through the pain of a marriage breakdown, I will be a very happy person.

We need to start with love, not just an ideal, but as something very real in our life. It is the only way to have a fulfilling life and marriage. Make love the bookends of your life.

Love.

Bookends.

To know is to love.

Get to know.

Love.

TEN TYPES OF RELATIONSHIPS THAT WON'T WORK

1.   Your relationship is all one way.

Is he into you more than you are into him? Or vice versa?

"Love endures long and is patient and kind; love never is envious nor boils over with jealousy, is not boastful or vainglorious, does not display itself haughtily."
[one corinthians chapter thirteen verse four]

Perhaps you currently have a love interest with whom you are head over heels in love, yet he does not give you much of the time of day, except for using your time of your day. If that's the case, your relationship is not reciprocal. The Word of God says, "Love is never jealous, or boils over with envy." How do jealousy and envy creep into a relationship? They creep in when the two people are not on the same page. If you are into him, and he is not into you, how do you think you're going to feel when someone comes up alongside him that he has eyes for? You are going to be open to jealousy and envy creeping into your life.

You deserve somebody who is as into you as you are into them. Many marriages have been destroyed because of jealousy, or where somebody has married somebody out of obligation. "I married him because he asked me." That kind of relationship is unlikely to last the test of time.

The "lean of faith" is somewhat of an art form. That is what I encourage women to do when exploring the possibilities of a new relationship. Lean towards the person but don't fall … on your face. I remember talking to my daughter Rachel, and I've watched some of the girls who have had an interest in guys, who have leaned. They haven't fallen for them, but they have leaned towards them. Leaning is safer than falling, but sometimes even leaning is painful as it requires enquiry, and sometimes as one person leans to enquire of the other, the response is upright rather than a mutual lean.

The matchmakers in all of us cheer, "Come on! That should work! They should like each other!" At the end of the day, my perspective is that you deserve somebody who is completely into you. If a guy isn't into you and the relationship is a one-way relationship, then that is a relationship that won't work.

You won't want to marry "that."

You truly deserve so much more.

My husband Jonathan is so into me, it's embarrassing. Seriously! It's somewhat embarrassing. I can't imagine being married to somebody if I was continually wondering whether they even liked me anymore or thought I was half attractive. He loves me, is into me, and we don't have any jealousy in our relationship. Women have tried to work their way into my husband's life because he is a leader and women can be attracted to that. It always amuses me, because there's no reaction in me at all. None; except that I feel sorry for the person, because it's embarrassing for them.

2.   You are in love with your partner's potential.

You only love him for who you dream he could become in the future and not who he is right now.

"It [love] is not conceited (arrogant and inflated with pride); it is not rude (unmannerly) and does not act unbecomingly. Love (God's love in us) does not insist on its own rights or its own way, for it is not self-seeking; it is not touchy or fretful or resentful; it takes no account of the evil done to it [it pays no attention to a suffered wrong]."
[one corinthians chapter thirteen verse five]

You're in love with his potential. You're only in love with him for whom you dream he could become in the future. It helps you deal with who he is right now. Let's move onto the next verse, verse 5. That is all sequential and not by accident. Verse 5 says, "It, love, is not conceited, it is not arrogant, inflated with pride. It is not rude, unmannerly, and does not act unbecomingly. Love, God's love in us, does not insist on its own rights, its own way. It is not self-seeking; it is not touchy or fretful, or resentful, it takes no account of the evil done to it, it pays no attention to a suffered wrong." Now, there's a tall order! Tuck that one away, because it is a good measuring gauge. If he is "full of himself" or rude, don't think for one second you going to be able to deal with that. You are going to tire of that fast. The Bible has this instruction for us, so that we can know actually who we are and recognize our value. We will shortchange our value if we are left to ourselves. We always do. And so, does he need to be Mr. Perfect? No, he does not, but it's important that he does not conduct himself in an unmannerly way. How many friends do you have who have boyfriends that are jerks? Rude. Unmannerly. Unbecomingly insisting on their way. It's their way or no way. We need to help these guys understand that we know we are worth more than that. We need to help our male friends understand that they are worth more than that.

Women's lives can be destroyed when they think they can change the man they are dating by marrying him. They sincerely – and mistakenly – believe they can help him become a nice person. Is that your mission in life? Do you really want to spend 50 years together with him as your special project? There is nothing wrong with a guy who opens the door and pays a bill, as in, you've had dinner, and he picks up the check for the two of you. There's nothing wrong with that. Some women have burnt their bras in the name of freedom, but for the sake of all of us, please put your bra back on! Understand that the reason you need to wear a bra is because God created you female, and we don't need to be the same as men! Women are of a different essence altogether. Maybe you've asked yourself, "Am I being demanding by expecting somebody to be nice?" No. This needs to be established at the beginning as your first bookend. I'm going to start this way, and it's going to be nice. Even if he doesn't open the door three months later, he did open the door once, which tells me he can do it again. It's when he's never done it before but rather wants you to be the door opener you should beware!

3.   He is your social justice project.

He wants the injustices and justified unrighteousness of his life embraced by you.

"It does not rejoice at injustice and unrighteousness, but rejoices when right and truth prevail."
[one corinthians chapter thirteen verse six]

He is your social justice project. He wants the injustices, and justified unrighteousness of his life embraced by you. He wants you to just love him. These guys are out there, waiting for you and your kind, merciful heart. He wants you, and he thinks that you should look after him because of all that he has been through. Verse six says this, "Love does not rejoice at injustice and unrighteousness, but rejoices when right and truth prevail." The problem is not so much that an injustice might have happened to him; the problem is when he will not embrace the truth, and do what is right. Maybe you are trying to help him read and believe what the Bible says about overcoming negative thoughts by renewing his mind. Perhaps you are trying to help him understand, but he just wants you to embrace his sense of injustice. If you're not careful, that can become your project for life.

We need to start at this point called love. The two of you need to be on the same page; completely sold out to being part of the solution together. When it comes to the injustices of the earth and his personal misfortune, you are not responsible for his healing and wholeness.

No one needs to marry somebody who wants you to make them your personal mission in life, for the rest of your life.

4.   You put him on a pedestal or even worse; he puts you on one!

There will be mighty disappointments when you realize that you can't live up, bear up and shut up, without "weakening!"

"Love bears up under anything and everything that comes, is ever ready to believe the best of every person, its hopes are fadeless under all circumstances, and it endures everything [without weakening]."

[one corinthians chapter thirteen verse seven]

You put him on a pedestal, or, even worse, he puts you on one. Would you want to be on a pedestal, or are you all too aware of your own human frailty? One thing worse than putting someone else on a pedestal, would be that somebody would put be me on one. Please don't do that to me, or yourself. I cannot maintain that position. I will fall off. In fact, I'm already climbing down; I do not belong there. It is not my place. I am a human being. It does not excuse me and does not give me cause to devalue grace in my life. There is one thing is for sure: Jesus Christ Himself is the only Person who can maintain position on that pedestal in my life, and He needs to be the only one on a pedestal in your life as well.

When someone puts us on a pedestal, there is an expectation that we would bear up and that we would live up to. The pedestal of perfection is not a soapbox for airing our opinions and getting our own way. It's a place of complete silence. We know we cannot live up to that, so we should not put him up there either. Love bears up under anything and everything. Let's determine not to put burdens on others that we know we cannot bear ourselves.

When I met Jonathan, I remember feeling like he was the most beautiful man of God, teacher and Pastor. It was a difficult transition for me when I realized that this beautiful man was interested in me. Let's be real. There had to be some chemistry, so it wasn't as though the man and the woman just decided to get married. No, there was an awkward moment at the realization that he liked me.

He liked me.

HE.

Liked.

ME!

What was I going to do and how was I going to handle it? I resisted initially, because I had set him on the biggest pedestal. I had to give him permission to climb down and be able to engage with me. Otherwise, our relationship wouldn't exist. Some of you might be aware that God has a godly man for you, and perhaps you are completely enamored by the fact that he is so amazing, just like I was with Jonathan. Allow him down from the pedestal. Sometimes the girl falls for a man but doesn't know how to do that properly. It's because we put him up there on a pedestal, and we need to allow him to climb down.

5.   He is in love with you because you are HOT!

Guess what – hotness will fade!

"Love never fails [never fades out or becomes obsolete or comes to an end]. As for prophecy (the gift of interpreting the divine will and purpose), it will be fulfilled and pass away; as for tongues, they will be destroyed and cease; as for knowledge, it will pass away [it will lose its value and be superseded by truth]."

[one corinthians chapter thirteen verse eight]

He's in love with you because you are a hottie. You are really cute, stunningly beautiful with your lovely little figure. He likes your lovely figure, he wants to marry your lovely little figure, and he thinks you're absolutely gorgeous. It's important that he's attracted to you, but if that is the primary or only reason he is marrying you, then the minute you have a baby and put on three pounds, he may well criticize you for the next 20 years. Trust me, men are visual, and it's true, you do need to have physical chemistry. You're going to sleep with this person. There's got to be some chemistry there. So, hottie matters. It's part of the first bookend! Guess what happens when you're moving towards the latter bookend days? Hotness fades, and rightly so. We shouldn't need to try to hold on to our hotness as we age, trying to look 25 when we're 80. Can you imagine how funny we would look? Let's be free to age gracefully!

Ask yourself if what makes him think you are the best thing is something external. Maybe he likes you in certain outfits? Buyer beware! Before you fall for him, be sure of one thing: that he loves your soul. He loves your person; he loves your spirit, and that he understands that he will also lose his hotness, at the appropriate time in life! This is so important. Verse 8 says, "Love never fails. Love never fades out, or becomes obsolete." It never comes to an end." Just about everything else does fade. That is why love, the bookend, needs to be established in your life.

I put on large amounts of weight during every pregnancy (and afterwards), and I am so glad I am married to a kind man because I know some men wouldn't cope with my weight gain! When I'm pregnant, I grow to almost twice my size. Some men might say, "I did not sign up for that." We need to understand that love, the bookend, goes through all of those seasons. It's not an excuse for us to be not looking after ourselves as best we can, but there is nothing more demotivating for a woman than to be criticized by a man. It doesn't motivate you to want to do anything about it. It can make you want to shrink, and just die inside. That is why it's so great to have girlfriends around you to encourage you. If you're in that situation now, I want to encourage you that there is not one ugly woman reading this book – in fact you are gorgeous! In my eyes, and in God's eyes, you are beautiful. When I teach on Body & Soul, it is all about freedom from the inside out. My husband did not pressure me one iota to lose weight after my pregnancies. He didn't even help me to lose any weight! He's the opposite and would say, "Darling, have some chocolate." He would tell me, "You're beautiful, don't worry about it." Whereas I would think, "Oh, I don't need to hear that!" I need to hear, "Get in shape!"

6.   **You think you know he is right for you even if no one else does.**

Always verify your feelings, especially if you have known the person for less than five minutes.

"For our knowledge is fragmentary (incomplete and imperfect), and our prophecy (our teaching) is fragmentary (incomplete and imperfect)."
[one corinthians chapter thirteen verse nine]

You believe he is right for you, even when everyone else says he isn't. When people make choices, even when they pull the "God said!" card, it really doesn't work, because it has no power. The "God said!" card is just a card used by people to justify their decisions. It has no power because there is no authority and no submission involved in the

"God said!" statement unless God has spoken. The truth is, when God speaks to us in our hearts, His Voice never contradicts His Word – the Bible. As Pastors, God helps us lead people. It is a significant responsibility and therefore we can't play matchmaker. We don't tell people who to date or who to marry, and, if asked our opinion, we share it cautiously. Our prayer as Pastors is that people will be in a healthy community in church life, that they will be reading the Word of God and that they will be praying about their future. Unfortunately, there are many people who aren't prepared to stay on the dry dock, allowing them to be built by God. Instead, they insist on jumping into the deep, ill prepared for what may be ahead.

Then, as soon as they are drowning or are perhaps flung out of a speedboat relationship so that their partner can move on to an upgraded model, you know who they call? They call us. The Pastors. It is not our role as Pastors to interfere, ever. It is our role as Pastors to help and guide, when invited. Watching people make mistakes is part of life. Praying that they will exercise wisdom is all that we can do. It is worth waiting on the dry dock while God is building you and building your future partner. You are better off sitting out the rest of your days, understanding that Jesus Christ Himself is your bookends, than being messed around for decades with somebody who you are not meant to be with. I know that is difficult for people, really difficult. This is why many people do not exercise wisdom. Many people just jump in anyway because they want the marriage and a big wedding day, more than they want freedom for their whole life. It's frightening!

Whenever asked for my opinion on a relationship, I always reply with questions. If we don't arrive at conclusions ourselves, we will always be looking to people to tell us what to do. We need to be guided by the light of God's Word and the Holy Spirit when we make decisions.

"For our knowledge is fragmentary, it is imperfect and incomplete. And our prophecy, our teaching, fragmentary, incomplete, and imperfect." [one corinthians chapter thirteen verse nine]

Don't think you know everything. I don't know everything, and you don't know everything. When it comes to relationships, the Bible tells us that our "knowledge is fragmentary." Fragmented. Something's missing, broken, pulled apart. It is not complete. You can't have the full scoop on your own. That's why it is good to have people who you can talk with, to give you Godly advice and wisdom, not tell you what to do. When you ask for wise counsel, be prepared for wise counsel. Perhaps there is something that you don't know about the person you are falling in love with that you've yet to discover. Are you prepared for the truth? We need to be prepared to hear the truth. Truth doesn't mean the end of a relationship. Truth is how healthy relationships are built. The Bible says that there is wisdom in a multitude of counsel. We need to listen to people who know us, rather than to confide in people who might just tell us what we want to hear.

7.   **You wrote on a card to him, "You complete me."**

And he liked the thought of being all that you need!

"But when the complete and perfect (total) comes, the incomplete and imperfect will vanish away (become antiquated, void, and superseded)." [one corinthians chapter thirteen verse ten]

You wrote on a card to him, "You complete me," and he loved it. He loved the thought of being all that you need. There's a sign that the relationship is not going to work. If I wrote that to my husband, he'd say, "Get over it. That's Jesus' role." He might initially think, "Oh, how cute!" Be sure of one thing however, if I truly expected Jonathan to fill the void of my life that only Jesus can fulfill, he would send me straight to my Bible. My husband loves that I need him, but I need him to be my husband, not my Savior. The role of Savior is strictly reserved for my Jesus. When a man is expected to fulfill all of a woman's emotional needs, he is simply unable to.

Your husband will disappoint you from time to time – he is not perfect. There should always be a big space for Jesus. Jonathan leaves me plenty of room for Jesus in my life. Seriously. Perhaps you have an amazing husband who disappoints you every now and again. Congratulations. Disappointment is normal because we are human. We need to learn to raise our tolerance and lower our expectations, and allow plenty of room for the Holy Spirit to move in our relationships. If you are in a relationship where there is no disappointment, because he is somehow fulfilling all of that, be concerned. There should be plenty of room for him to be very human and occasionally upset you so that you go to Jesus, who should be a real big man in your life. That is a good thing!

8.   He is a 15 year old in a 25-year-old body.

Do you really want to sign up to parent him?

"When I was a child, I talked like a child, I thought like a child, I reasoned like a child; now that I have become a man, I am done with childish ways and have put them aside."
[one corinthians chapter thirteen verse eleven]

He is a 15-year-old boy in a 25-year-old body. The Bible says, verse 11 of 1 Corinthians 13, "When I was a child I talked like a child, I thought like a child, I reasoned like a child. Now that I have become a man I have done away with childish things, and I have put them aside." Let me ask you a question: do you really want to parent him?

Do you really want to parent him? You might think you do because you're longing to look after somebody, but parenting a man-child? It just sounds wrong! Man-child. It sounds wrong, because it is wrong.

I had an interesting experience happen to me once when I was visiting my homeland Australia. I was sitting at a domestic airport terminal, waiting to get on a flight from Sydney to Adelaide to Melbourne. I was going to Melbourne to speak at a church. I was sitting waiting to board the plane, and I was on the phone, talking to my husband, Jonathan. I had my travel bag beside me, and I had my Bible on my lap. I love to read my Bible when I'm traveling. Then a young guy came and sat down right next to me, when he could have sat anywhere else. The seat beside me was not the last available seat in the terminal lounge. This guy would have been somewhere in his early 20s. I was determined not to look at him because of the creepy vibe I was getting. So I was sitting there, minding my business, when all of a sudden the guy pulls out a big sketchbook. As I looked around the lounge, I caught a glimpse of what he was drawing on his big sketchbook – he was drawing a big picture of a woman in a teeny, weeny bikini. Charming! "Oh, wow," I thought to myself, "that you would pull that out here, and feel to do that right in my space." Yuck! He was creeping me out. Next thing I knew, he had turned his head and was looking at me.

I was incredulous.

Could not believe it.

He then turned his sketchbook page over and he started to draw me! I'm thinking, "You creep!" It was just rude. It was creepy, and it was rude. I picked up my belongings because the plane was about to board, and went for a walk to the other side of the departure lounge, where there was a staff member at the ticket counter. As I stood at that counter, I was so irritated that this silly boy had been sketching me. I looked back over to where I had been sitting, and he was gone. I needed to know where he was – just as if you had lost a big creepy spider in your house, you would want to know where it had gone. So I turned to the right and there he was, staring at me still! He didn't know who he was messing with at this point, obviously.

At this stage I'm thinking, "I've got to get on this plane, I don't know what his problem is, but let's just say he has one. I didn't want to be on a plane, 36,000 feet in the air, with this guy and his problem. So I spoke quietly to a staff member at the check-in counter. As softly as I could, I whispered, "There is a guy following me. He sat next to me, and has been creeping me out, and now he's following me, and he's getting on this plane! I don't know what to do, I'm really embarrassed, and I'm sorry that I'm even mentioning it, but I don't know what to do!" And he said, "Okay where is he?" and I thought, "Oh, my gosh! I can't say where he is, because I don't know what this is going to look like or what's going to happen."

I was very embarrassed, and the airline staff kindly allowed me to board the plane around the other side. As I sat there on the plane I realized, "Creepy guy is about to get on this plane, so I need to say something to the flight attendant." I summoned the courage to say something to the flight attendant, and then the guy boarded the plane and was seated in the back. I was seated at the front of the plane. Next thing I knew, he got up, and he began drawing, furiously. Drawing, drawing, drawing. The flight attendant said to me, "Don't worry ma'am, we will take care of it, and we will be watching him." These two flight attendants from the back of the cabin came up, and said, "21 Foxtrot, we're watching him."

He was disturbing.

I was just trying to get to my destination.

I received a message from the captain of the flight via one of the flight attendants saying, "The captain thinks you should call your husband as soon as we touch down." I did not want to call my husband. I was in Australia and he was in America. They asked who would be meeting me at the airport, and when they found out that no one would be meeting me at the airport they told me they would give me a full crew escort off the plane. The plane disembarked; and the creepy guy walked past and got off. Then the captain and crew took me off the plane and escorted me to my connecting flight. What happened could have been worse. Women are violated all the time. Thankfully nothing happened to me. Maybe you have had inappropriate encounters with men. All men are not the same, but some guys never grow up and you don't want to embark on a relationship with a boy or a guy who has not made the transition from a child or adolescent to a man.

9.   You actually believe he is perfect!

Oh really???

"For now we are looking in a mirror that gives only a dim (blurred) reflection [of reality as in a riddle or enigma], but then [when perfection comes] we shall see in reality and face to face! Now I know in part (imperfectly), but then I shall know and understand fully and clearly, even in the same manner as I have been fully and clearly known and understood [by God]."
[one corinthians chapter thirteen verse twelve]

You actually believe he is perfect. If you marry that idea, you are going to be disappointed, if not by your wedding night, maybe the next day. I don't mean that in a crass way. We're girls and some of us live in fairyland. Cinderella in her little bubble, on her wedding day, where it's all about the dress and the hair. A woman loves to plan her wedding, and a man loves to plan his wedding night! And it's just one of those things. It's a reality of life, most beautiful union, fantastic, wonderful, but guess what? The wedding night may not be perfect. Some people think, "Okay, I guess that's the way life's going to be, for the rest of my life." I can assure you that a healthy marriage gets better and better.

If you are dating somebody and you haven't had your first fight, keep dating until you have. When my daughter Rachel was dating her now-husband Jamin, I couldn't wait until they had their first fight! I know that might surprise some of you, but I was worried. Rachel and Jamin are about as close to perfect as they come as far as being lovely people and least likely to get into it, fight-wise. Because they hadn't ever had a real fight, I thought, "Oh my gosh, they're in delusional la-la land about the fact that they're going to, and they could actually keep this little facade going for quite some time. Maybe into eternity." It had to happen. And it did happen, and I was relieved. I thought, "Now you are ready to get married!"

That may seem controversial, but I believe we need something to fight for in life. How boring life is when there is no friction, there is no challenge, there's no opinion, there's no interaction, there's no sense of working it out, how boring! I'm not suggesting that we should be intentionally controversial or fight over things that don't matter, but healthy debate about important matters helps strengthen our relationships.

If you believe he is perfect, that is what verse 12 says, "For we know we are looking into a mirror now, that gives only a dim, a blurred reflection of reality. But then we shall see in reality, face to face, now I know in part, but then I shall know and fully know." When it comes to our partner, you can be confident in this: you're not going to see perfection on this side of eternity because the Word of God says that there are wonderful things promised to us... later. We will see it in the image of Christ, not in the image of our husband. We need to stay focused on that.

10. Your relationship with God is enough for the two of you.

His conviction is you, and your conviction is God.

"And so faith, hope, love abide [faith--conviction and belief respecting man's relation to God and divine things; hope--joyful and confident expectation of eternal salvation; love--true affection for God and man, growing out of God's love for and in us], these three; but the greatest of these is love."

[one corinthians chapter thirteen verse thirteen]

Your relationship with God is enough for the two of you. Really? His conviction is you, but your conviction is God. If his conviction is you, but your conviction is God, this type of relationship will not work and has no longevity to it, because your conviction in God is not going to go away. You can try to suppress it as much as you like, but it will haunt you for the rest of your life. The man you marry will need to have his own relationship with God to be strong. That means embracing the Trinity: God the Father – all-knowing, all-powerful, ever-present; Jesus – Lord and Savior; Holy Spirit – Comforter and Convictor.

To be "unequally yoked" is not simply about a Christian being with a non-Christian, it's also about two Christians who are not on the same page when it comes to life values. Marriage, ministry, money, etc. So when it comes to being equally yoked, it is important to find out if you are on the same page about everything that matters most to you. How are you going to discipline your children? How are you going to spend your Christmas? How are you going to spend money? What happens when all of a sudden you realize how different you are? Your relationship with God is not enough for the two of you. He needs his own personal relationship with God, and so do you. When you have the same values and convictions, you have a strong foundation on which to build your relationship.

chapter seven

seven signs that he is mr. wrong

wrong

wrong

wrong

boys

"Boys will be boys, and so will a lot of middle-aged men."[1]

Kin Hubbard

What is obvious to everyone else around us is not always obvious to us. It is good to observe some behaviors that may be obvious to your family and friends, but overlooked by you. Let's take off the rose colored glasses for a few moments as we determine whether he is a boy, a guy or a man. There are so many different variables on this subject, but for those of you who have not walked down the aisle yet, carefully consider these seven qualities of Mr. Wrong, and choose wisely!

7 SIGNS THAT HE IS MR. WRONG

1.   He needs anger management!

He lets fly over anything! Little or big, he has very little self-control. How do I know that he's not going to be right for me? Apart from the fact it should be obvious, unfortunately, it's not for some women. Some women think that he's just a man who needs to eat a decent meal. He's just a man whose sugar levels are low, he just needs me to feed him and then he won't be angry anymore. Don't mind me for being facetious, because at the end of the day he lacks one very special quality, which is found in this verse below:

> "But the Holy Spirit produces this kind of fruit in our lives: love, joy, peace, patience, kindness, goodness, faithfulness, gentleness, and self-control. There is no law against these things!"
> [galatians chapter five verse twenty-two to twenty-three]

Therefore, if you are leaning, and have even fallen for somebody who cannot control his temper, don't think for one second you are going to be able to solve that issue yourself. So what happens if Mr. Man needs anger management? He has to want you more than he wants the freedom to indulge his temper. If he really wants you, you will see some Fruit of the Spirit in his life. You are worth more than that, and these keys are to help rescue those who have not yet walked down the aisle. Perhaps you have walked down the aisle already, and you are thinking "But what if he wasn't angry until after we got married?" Maybe his anger is somehow related to his relationship with you, but then again maybe it isn't. Perhaps he learned to keep his anger under control until he felt safe to let roar.

2.   He is a control freak.

The second sign that he, this boy, guy, not-quite-a-man is Mr. Wrong, is that he is a control freak. Does this really need an explanation? We should be able to readily identify a control freak. A control freak wants to control you, and will weigh in with his opinion on what you think, do or say, and tell you that he knows better than you when it comes to what is best for your life. He might tell you what to wear, what to eat, what to think, and what to say. He might insist on being "in charge" all the time. Sometimes we might think that kind of behavior is normal, or that it is what strong leadership looks like. You need to know that it is controlling behavior, and that it is not normal or healthy. I love my husband and I am submitted to his leadership. It's important to know that healthy leadership is not controlling.

> "Christ has set us free to live a free life. So take your stand! Never again let anyone put a harness of slavery on you."
> [galatians chapter five verse one]

Control freaks love to isolate their women so that they can be the little king in a little manmade kingdom. When a guy tells you what to think, what to wear, what to say, what not to do, who to hang with, that you don't need your family anymore, you just need him - he is very clearly Mr. Wrong and therefore not right for you.

3.   He is a victim.

Another sign that this boy, guy, not-quite-a-man is Mr. Wrong is that he consistently sees himself as a victim. He blames everyone except himself for everything bad that has ever happened, that is happening now, or that will happen in his future. Would you like some cheese with that whine?

> "Therefore, if anyone is in Christ, he is a new creation; old things have passed away; behold, all things have become new,"
> [two corinthians chapter five verse seventeen]

Sometimes we read the Word of God, and we think, wouldn't that be nice? We can think that this is idealistic and stop there, or we can believe in the Word of God and learn to stand on God's Word. We've got to remember, whether this relates to us having had a terrible past or whether this relates to our potential suitor's past, that our past is not there to be brought along for the ride. Maybe he was a victim to something once, but that doesn't mean he has to be a victim to it now, and it certainly doesn't mean he has to take it with him into his future - or into your future for that matter. What part of that do you need to co-sign? We love Mr. Victim but we want Mr. Victim to get help. We don't help him by marrying him.

4.   He needs to live in a cold shower.

The fourth sign that this boy, guy, not-quite-a-man is Mr. Wrong, is that he needs to live in a cold shower because he lacks sexual integrity, or he has sexual addictions. Did I really just say that? Yes, I did. We all live in the real world. Please don't think you are going to be able to change this about him if he is the kind of guy that needs to live in a cold shower. It doesn't mean that God can't help him change, but you are not God.

You are not God.

That should be a relief.

That is why we have offered a course at our church called Valiant Man, that teaches guys what to do with their eyes when they go to the beach. That's helpful, because that guy at the beach is one day going to be someone's husband. Have you ever had some guy, with his big old wedding ring on, treat you like a piece of meat? He was someone's boyfriend once, and that person decided to marry him. Those of us who have not walked down the aisle yet still have an opportunity to say, "Oh wow, I so do not need that in my life."

Sexual addiction, promiscuity, and a lack of sexual integrity are very real and widespread problems. It is not something isolated to just a few people. It is right there for all guys to live in if they so choose. Don't go blindly into a relationship with a guy thinking and hoping that this is not a problem. You've got to know if they have an issue in this area, and you know that by leaning in for a long time, by observing, by knowing family, by knowing friends. How does he spend his spare time? Go to the beach and see where he glances, where he looks and where he stares! Don't presume that because he's such a nice guy that he couldn't possibly have a problem with sexual integrity or addiction.

There is, however, always good news found in the Word of God.

For all the guys that may feel that they've tried everything yet nothing helps, there is hope! Listen to this, "The answer, thank God, is that Jesus Christ can and does."

> "I've tried everything and nothing helps. I'm at the end of my rope. Is there no one who can do anything for me? Isn't that the real question? The answer, thank God, is that Jesus Christ can and does. He acted to set things right in this life of contradictions where I

want to serve God with all my heart and mind, but am pulled by the influence of sin to do something totally different."

[romans chapter seven verses twenty-four to twenty-five]

That does not have to be a sentence over anyone's life.

Women can be naive about this subject. We can just presume that it will not happen to us. We can presume that they will not be like that. We can presume just because they flirted with us in the first place that they won't flirt with somebody else later. Flirts are a whole other situation. If he flirted with you to get your attention, there's probably a pattern somewhere. Value yourself more than that. Do not be attracted to and impressed by a flirt. When they tell you that you have the most beautiful eyes, the most anointed voice and the most stunning hair. Simply respond with a smile and walk away.

Walk away.

5.   He is a boy, and that's not cute anymore!

The fifth sign that this boy, guy, not-quite-a-man is Mr. Wrong is that he has not grown up, and you feel like his mother because he still needs looking after. He is a boy – and that's not cute anymore!

"When I was a child, I talked like a child, I thought like a child, I reasoned like a child. When I became a man, I put childish ways behind me."

[one corinthians chapter thirteen verse eleven]

If he is selfish, moody, intent on getting his own way, won't play in the sand if it's not about him, then back it up and walk away until he decides to be a man. It's time to observe, from a distance. Does his attention match his intentions? Is he willing to become a man of integrity: knowing right and doing right?

6.   He is always "out to lunch".

A sixth sign that this boy, guy, not-quite-a-man is Mr. Wrong is that he is always out to lunch. He is emotionally unavailable and unpredictable and frequents his "nothing box" a little too often. (A place where he decompresses on his own, doing nothing!) When my husband Jonathan is in his nothing box, I know that even if I am sitting next to him, I could even be holding his hand, if he's in his nothing box, that's his nothing box. There's no entry point; there's no door. There's not even a window! I wouldn't even know how to get in there if I tried. So I don't even go there. But if my husband lived in his nothing box we'd have no relationship. Sometimes guys can be intense and emotionally connected initially, and then be all about needing their personal space later. Before you've even walked down the aisle, you want to know that you are with somebody you can connect with emotionally, not just initially over a passionate first few months, but for the long run. That is not simply about that fact that you're a woman, and you're an emotional being. When you're a little old lady, and he's a little old man, guess what's going to matter?

Your soul.

You need to find your soul mate, because when you are 95 in the shade, wrinkled up like a prune in your latter years, that is going to be about all that matters.

> "I will give you a new heart and put a new spirit in you; I will remove from you your heart of stone and give you a heart of flesh."
>
> [ezekiel chapter thirty-six verse twenty-six]

Men who have a heart of stone need to come into contact with the real and living God, who wants to take that stony, cold, heart away and put in a heart of flesh.

7.   He is allergic to hard work.

He spends a lot of time thinking about what he wants to do with all the money he does not have, rather than working hard. This is what the Bible says,

> "Lazy hands make a man poor, but diligent hands bring wealth. He who gathers crops in summer is a wise son, but he who sleeps during harvest is a disgraceful son."
>
> [proverbs chapter ten verses four and five]

Diligent hands bring wealth. Wealth is not simply making ends meet. The Bible is clear; diligent hands bring wealth. Wealth is abundance; wealth is blessing, wealth is enough for me and you and other people. Diligent hands. You want to find out what he is doing with those hands. He's either sitting on them, or he's using them.

If you have not walked down the aisle yet, it's important in your leaning process to find out what he really does with his time, talent and treasure. Go ahead and inspect what you expect.

Go ahead.

greatness

"Man becomes great exactly in the degree in which he works for the welfare of his fellow-men."[2]

Mahatma Gandhi

chapter eight

five time bombs that may destroy a relationship

destroy

destroy

destroy

Healthy relationships don't just happen. They require commitment and investment. Even the healthiest relationships can come under strain during different seasons in life. The good news is, the healthier your relationship is, the more likely you are to be able to weather the storms that may come your way. Sometimes, we can be lured into thinking that we can enter a relationship that is a potential time bomb without it affecting us. Time bombs exist, and they have the potential to explode. There are certain relationships that are more challenging than others, and it is important to realize what those challenges are so that you can count the cost and choose wisely.

5 TIME BOMBS THAT MAY DESTROY A RELATIONSHIP

1.   **Significant age difference, of more than ten years.**
        [the generation leap]

My husband is twelve years older than me. When we married I promised him that he would have my immaturity as his constant companion for the rest of his life, as I would always be twelve years his junior! I do try my best to grow and learn in maturity, but the reality is, I am over a decade younger, and I think differently and have different taste in many areas. We are on the same page with all of the important things in our marriage, such as our purpose, our children, and our family. When it comes to taste in music, however, this is where we see the gap! I love the eighties, and he loves the seventies. I love disco and pop, and he loves Pink Floyd and The Who. Age difference does matter and especially if you are looking to date someone who is ten years or more your junior and you are a female! Go slowly and carefully as age difference is a potential time bomb that could go off ... tick, tick, tick, boom!

2.   Different spiritual conviction.

[when either of you are not of the same faith]

You can't change your partner. Having personal convictions about what you believe is important, and respecting the personal convictions and beliefs of your partner is just as important. Being Christians doesn't necessarily mean that you are equally yoked. Many Christians believe many different things about God, about what His Word means to them, about going to church, about raising kids. It is hard enough building a healthy relationship when you are on the same page in your spiritual life, let alone trying to hope for some health in your relationship when you don't even believe the same things. It might be wisdom now to call it a day, and walk away before you say, "I do!" Or else, tick, tick, tick, boom!

3.   Different ethnic and social backgrounds.

[blue collar vs. white collar; upper crust vs. down and out]

Coming from different ethnic and social backgrounds is not necessarily going to be a problem in your relationship, as long as you spend adequate time prior to committing to marriage. It is important to get to know each other, each other's families and talk through all possible implications. Communication is key here. It's when the pressure is on that issues tend to surface and potentially explode. You need to know who you are and what you value in your culture and the way were raised. And you need to give your partner time and space to express how he sees your relationship working in the future. One of the greatest time bomb subjects in any marriage relationship is "money," so if you have come from different financial backgrounds, this has the potential to be explosive. If you love to spend and he loves to scrimp and save ... tick, tick, tick, boom!

4.   Overbearing In-laws.

[is he prepared to "leave and cleave"?]

You can't choose your family, and you can't choose your husband's family. They will always be part of your life, so the sooner you observe your potential partner's interaction with his mother and father, the sooner you will know if he is going to be able to cut the apron strings. Healthy involvement is one thing, but unhealthy co-dependence has destroyed many relationships. The Bible says that he should leave his parents and cleave to his wife. That is his responsibility, even if his parents don't want to make the cut. That is essential for a healthy marriage relationship. Boundaries are important, and they need to be established, otherwise ... tick, tick, tick, boom!

5.   Long distance relationship.

[especially if there is no trust and commitment]

Long distance relationships can work, but they can also be problematic. There are many factors to take into consideration. If you both already know each other and began dating just before moving away from each other, then at least you know each other. It is difficult to get to know someone in a remote relationship. The biggest key is to stay connected, stay authentic and stay committed. If you are in love with someone who lives in a different state or a different country, be sure that the love is reciprocal and not just one way. Ask yourself some tough but important questions, such as, "Do I trust him?" and "Is he really committed to me?" If you aren't sure, speak up! Go there. Have a conversation. With technology, you can talk face to face from across the world. Geography may not be a problem, or it may. Just be sure to be on the same page regardless of geography, otherwise ... tick, tick, tick, boom!

wisdom

"Don't develop partnerships with those who are not
followers of Jesus' teachings. For what real connection
can exist between righteousness and rebellion? How
can light participate in darkness?"

two corinthians chapter six verse fourteen
[the voice]

reality

"The only time a woman really succeeds in changing a man is when he is a baby."[1]

Natalie Wood

chapter nine

eight qualities to look for in a life partner

look

look

look

Shared values are more important than shared interests.

My husband and I have many different interests and passions. Some that we share are: church, family, food, travel, home, TV and cooking shows! In other areas, it could seem that we might be incompatible. After all, my husband loves sports and can watch multiple hours of sport on TV. I would rather watch wet paint dry! I love to shop even if I don't buy anything, but my husband would rather tend his garden vegetables than spend hours shopping!

My husband loves history and is great at all things financial.

I love dreaming about the future, and strategizing our calendar.

The amazing thing is; our differences unite us. Regardless of how we spend our spare time, we have an incredibly strong relationship. That's because our shared values are more important than our shared interests.

Values are our "rules of life" that are inherently important to us. They are personal beliefs that are a fundamental part of who you are, and they tend to be consistent throughout your life, unless something major happens that causes you to change them. Most people keep the values instilled in them as children.

Your values are vital in your life including the choices you make, how you react or respond to situations, who you spend time with and the boundaries you set. We always appreciate when our values are respected, and we, usually feel uncomfortable when anyone disrespects our values. Values are an important part of who we are and matching those values is the first step in establishing whether a potential partner is right for you. A lack of shared values is many times the basis of ongoing frustration and arguments. Ultimately, a lack of shared values can cause a total breakdown in your relationship.

Although you and your partner don't need to have exactly the same values, it's important to for you to establish what your main values are. Knowing your values is also important if you are single, and looking for your life partner. You'll kiss a lot more frogs if you keep dating people without first knowing your personal values. You need to know your values so that you can find your match!

There are three main reasons why my relationship with my husband works so well, despite our differences.

1.   Time.

The first reason is that we prioritize time together doing what we both enjoy, such as spending time as a family, going on dates, and enjoying endless conversations with friends.

2.   Respect.

The second reason is that we each respect how different the other is. Rather than feeling as though need to find more in common, we love the fact that we both have different interests, and allow each other the space to be unique.

3.   Purpose.

The third and main reason our relationship works so well, despite being quite different, is because of our shared purpose.

Having shared interests is important. It is wonderful to be with someone who is interested in what interests you, and vice versa, but the most important element in a healthy relationship is shared values. These shared values will strengthen the foundation of your relationship enormously. Values are just one of at least seven other qualities to look for in a partner for life.

EIGHT QUALITIES TO LOOK FOR IN A LIFE PARTNER

1.   Values.

You are in the same sentence, in the same paragraph, in the same chapter, on the same page, in the same book.

"Do not be unequally yoked with unbelievers   [do not make mismatched alliances with them or come under a different yoke with them, inconsistent with your faith]. For what partnership have right living and right standing with God with iniquity and lawlessness? Or how can light have fellowship with darkness?"

[two corinthians chapter six verse fourteen]

2.   Teachability.

You and he are teachable and committed to growing spiritually and mentally.

"Instead of claiming to know what God says, ask questions of one another, such as 'How do we understand God in this?' But don't go around pretending to know it all, saying 'God told me this...God told me that....' I don't want to hear it anymore. Only the person I authorize speaks for me. Otherwise, my Message gets twisted, the Message of the living God-of-the-Angel-Armies."

[jeremiah chapter twenty-three verses thirty-five and thirty-six]

3.   Emotional openness.

You are both able to be vulnerable with each other, without fear of repercussion. You guard not only your own heart, but choose to guard each other's hearts too.

"Above all else, guard your heart, for everything you do flows from it."
[proverbs chapter four verse twenty-three]

4.   Integrity.

You both know right and do right.

"The man of integrity walks securely, but he who takes crooked paths will be found out."
[proverbs chapter ten verse nine]

5.   Identity.

You both have a healthy self-esteem and both live in approval, not rejection.

"So God created man in His own image, in the image and likeness of God He created him; male and female He created them. And God blessed them and said to them, "Be fruitful, multiply, and fill the earth, and subdue it [using all its vast resources in the service of God and man]; and have dominion over the fish of the sea, the birds of the air, and over every living creature that moves upon the earth..." And God saw everything that He had made, and behold, it was very good (suitable, pleasant) and He approved it completely. And there was evening and there was morning, a sixth day."
[genesis chapter one verses twenty-seven to thirty-one]

6.   Maturity and responsibility.

You are both committed to giving 100% so that there are no gaps. No healthy relationship is built on 50/50 contributions. If you both to try to give 100% and one of you is having a bad day, then there will be enough emotional equity in the bank for you to get through and move forward. If you only live at minimum contribution levels, you will always be in danger of a deficit.

"God spoke: "Let us make human beings in our image, make them reflecting our nature so they can be responsible for the fish in the sea, the birds in the air, the cattle, and, yes, Earth itself, and every animal that moves on the face of Earth." God created human beings; He created them godlike, reflecting God's nature. He created them male and female. God blessed them: "Prosper! Reproduce! Fill Earth! Take charge! Be responsible…""
[genesis chapter one verses twenty-six to twenty-eight]

7. Positive attitude towards life.

You both understand that crisis can mean both opportunity and danger.

"Do not be conformed to this world (this age), [fashioned after and adapted to its external, superficial customs], but be transformed (changed) by the [entire] renewal of your mind [by its new ideals and its new attitude], so that you may prove [for yourselves] what is the good and acceptable and perfect will of God, even the thing which is good and acceptable and perfect [in His sight for you]."
[romans chapter twelve verse two]

8. Personal chemistry.

You can find all seven in common, but this eighth key is key. Chemistry is what draws you to each other in the first place and holds you together for a lifetime.

"Kiss me – full on the mouth! Yes! For your love is better than wine, headier than your aromatic oils."

[song of solomon chapter one verses two to five]

Chemistry is more than a physical attraction; it's attitude and passion for life. It's a whole combination of intelligence, sexuality and an emotional connection to the other person.

There are basically four areas of chemistry:

1. **Physical.**
   Physical chemistry generates desire.

2. **Emotional.**
   Emotional chemistry generates affection.

3. **Mental.**
   Mental chemistry creates interest.

4. **Spiritual.**
   Spiritual chemistry creates love.

A soul mate includes all four.
A soul mate is your bookend friend.
Bookend friend.
For life.

direction

"Love does not consist in gazing at each other, but in looking outward together in the same direction."[1]

Antoine de Saint-Exupery

chapter ten

chemistry + call + construction

all 3 c's

all 3 c's

all 3 c's

This chapter [written by my husband Jonathan] will help us build a healthy marriage relationship while understanding the power of a three-fold cord that is not easily broken. The three components are as follows:

1. **Chemistry**
   [passion]

2. **Call**
   [purpose]

3. **Construction**
   [plan]

God is a God of relationship. Christianity is not a religion of observing rules and regulations. It is a relationship with God that transforms every other relationship.

We live in a world full of dysfunction and broken relationships. We all come from homes that have experienced some form of relational breakdown, divorce, conflict, abuse and alienation. You might think that yours is the only dysfunctional family, but it's not! Every single family has to deal with the reality of relational dysfunction.

Even Jesus was born into a complicated family situation, in a dysfunctional environment. His mother conceived him out of wedlock; he had two fathers, a stepfather, Joseph, and a heavenly father, God. He had half-brothers and half-sisters, and He lived in a village where people gossiped and whispered about the circumstances of His birth. So Jesus identifies with us completely in all of the complexities, issues and realities that you and I face in our relationships.

Over the years, I've observed in other people's relationships and in my own, that relationships can bring some of the greatest joy and blessing to our lives, but they can also bring some of the greatest heartache and pain.

Because God is a God of relationship, His mission has always been to restore us to a right relationship with Himself and with each other.

Therefore, His Word is filled with wisdom and keys to building great relationships with Him and each other.

Choosing our life partner is no exception to this.

In Ecclesiastes 4:12 Solomon writes an interesting and profound truth, "A threefold cord is not quickly broken."

There are three recurring qualities of great relationships, particularly marriages that I have observed in the Word of God over and over again.

I believe that these three elements are keys to choosing our partner in life. When they are part of the equation of our marriage, our relationship like Solomon's "three-fold cord" will not be easily broken.

THREE INGREDIENTS OF A HEALTHY MARRIAGE

1.   Chemistry.

The first stage in any friendship or relationship that leads to marriage is "chemistry." When someone catches your attention, you notice someone that you would like to meet, or there's an initial attraction to an individual, that attraction is "chemistry". Chemistry attracts and draws us to each other in the first or Initial stage of any relationship.

Chemistry is not only a key element in attracting us to our partner in the initial stage of our relationship; it is also essential to keep and grow that chemistry in our marriage. It's what keeps the attraction and excitement in our relationship. We should have chemistry in our marriage because this is the only person on the planet that we can have this special kind of intimate chemistry and relationship with.

However, we will never build a relationship on chemistry alone. It's sad to say that the honeymoon with all of its chemistry is going to come to an end! We have to include other important ingredients to our relationship for it to grow. Healthy relationships move from chemistry to construction. To building a relationship, beyond the initial chemistry, with a deep commitment to constructing a relationship together that is going to have longevity.

2.   Call.

Jesus called His disciples to follow Him, which gave them a purpose for their lives. Paul the Apostle began his letters by writing, "Paul called to be an Apostle of Jesus Christ." which gave him his purpose in life. Paul writes, "we are called to belong to Jesus Christ," and "we are called according to His purpose," which gives us our purpose in life.

Our call gives us our purpose in life

One of the most important things in a relationship that flourishes is understanding the power of a common purpose.

In Amos 3:3 the Bible says, "How can two walk together unless they agree?" Here Amos is speaking a prophetic word to the nation of Israel. God speaks about his relationship with Israel as a marriage. In a relationship where there is proximity, two people cannot walk together unless they are in agreement. He was talking to the nation of Israel at time when they were not aligned with God in the way that they were living their lives. Essentially God was saying, "If you want to have a relationship with Me that is going to flourish, then you will need to align your purpose with My purpose."

In our marriage, Dianne and I want chemistry to be a continual part of our relationship. However, one of the most powerful things in our relationship is that our chemistry is combined with a common call and purpose that she and I share together.

We have a common call that is a common purpose that binds us together.

We realize that together, we're building God's Kingdom. We're building our lives, we're building a marriage, we're building a family, we're building our church and we're building all of this with a common purpose. Sometimes when you're going through a tough season, you experience moments when the chemistry might not be the kind of chemistry that you want. You might experience a more volatile kind of chemistry in which sparks fly! It's especially in those times that we appreciate the value and power of a common call and purpose.

The most powerful thing in those moments or difficult seasons is the common sense of purpose that we share that binds us together with God as a three-fold cord that cannot be easily broken.

If you are considering marriage or building a marriage that you want to flourish, make sure that you understand the power of agreement in building your relationship. Make sure you share a common call and purpose because a threefold cord is not easily broken.

3.   Construction.

A relationship begins with chemistry, but construction will determine its end.

Our relationship must graduate from chemistry to construction.

Any relationship that flourishes and is built to last must be constructed through the many seasons of life, through the good times and the tough times.

Jesus talked about the importance of construction and building on a sure foundation in such a way that our lives can stand whatever storms we encounter. He didn't say, "If the storms come." He said, "When the storms come." He spoke of the inevitability of tough times in life, in our relationships, in our marriage.

"Therefore whoever hears these sayings of Mine and does them, I will liken him to a wise man who built his house on the rock." Matthew 7:24 [NKJV]

"These words I speak to you are not incidental additions to your life, homeowner improvements to your standard of living. They are foundational words, words to build a life on. If you work these words into your life, you are like a smart carpenter who built his house on solid rock. Rain poured down; the river flooded, a tornado hit—but nothing moved that house. It was fixed to the rock." Matthew 7:24-25 [The Message]

It's not chemistry that sees us through these seasons it's construction.

Solomon writes, "The wise woman builds her house, but the foolish pulls it down with her hands." Proverbs 14:1 [NKJV]

What Solomon is saying is that our wisdom is demonstrated in our commitment to construction, our folly is demonstrated in being controlled by our feelings.

A threefold cord that is not easily broken requires chemistry, call and construction.

Chemistry.

Call.

Construction.

When all three of these are taken into consideration in choosing our life's partner, and they are built into the fabric of our marriage we will reap the rewards of that wisdom that builds our house.

A threefold cord is not easily broken.

Not.

Easily

Broken.

grow up

"Brothers and sisters, don't think like children. Be innocent of malice but mature in understanding."

one corinthians chapter fourteen verse twenty
[the voice]

defined

GIRL

A female child; a young or relatively young woman.

CHICK

A young woman; a female peer; the opposite sex to guys.

WOMAN

An adult female person, as distinguished from a girl or a man.

part three

girls chicks women

example

"A capable, intelligent, and virtuous woman – who is he who can find her? She is far more precious than jewels and her value is far above rubies or pearls. The heart of her husband trusts in her confidently and relies on and believes in her securely, so that he has no lack of [honest] gain or need of [dishonest] spoil. She comforts, encourages, and does him only good as long as there is life within her. She seeks out wool and flax and works with willing hands [to develop it]. She is like the merchant ships loaded with foodstuffs; she brings her household's food from a far [country]."

proverbs chapter thirty-one verses ten to fourteen
[amplified version]

I have always found it fascinating that the Bible describes the Proverbs 31 woman being likened to a merchant ship – fully loaded – so I decided to find out more about the largest moving vessels on Planet Earth. We get to choose what kind of vessel we are going to be – a merchant ship built for purpose or a cruise ship built for pleasure. Maybe you feel more like a runabout boat or a dinghy, or a ferry, doing the same thing day in, day out. However, God has designed and created you to be like a Merchant Ship, for His purpose.

We were never designed to provide pleasure for a passing cruising crowd. We were never designed to simply ferry our lives around without any sense of destiny. We were never designed to lug along without energy and advancement in our lives. And we were certainly not designed to speed through life at a pace that causes us to miss the meaning of life. God has designed and created you for purpose bigger and broader than you have imagined. You have been made on purpose for His purpose. You have been designed for capacity.

A merchant ship is not pretty, but it is full of purpose. We need to remember that merchant ships are not built in the ocean. They are built on dry docks. If you are not yet sailing your high seas and not yet experiencing the responsibility and seasickness that comes with your high seas, you are still on the dry dock. There is a reason for that. You might wonder why you are in this season. Just be assured God is building you and building your life. We need to say, "I am here because God is building something inside of me. God has need of me to learn some stuff. I'm not sailing the high seas because I am not ready to sail the high seas. The responsibility that comes with that is bigger than me, and I will sink."

Whether you are sailing oceans of opportunity in this season of your life, or feel as though you are being nailed or bolted together in the dry dock, remember that God has designed and created you for a purpose bigger and broader than you have imagined.

The dry dock is not punishment.

The dry dock is preparation.

Preparation!

We are born to be free. Think about how many times in a normal day you have an opportunity to shrink on the inside.

So back to the high seas.

Back to the dry dock.

It's not about breaking away from the dry dock ahead of time so we can sail the high seas and sink. It's about breaking away from the mindset that asks when I'm in the dry dock, "Am I here because I am being judged by God?" It is better for us to spend a lengthy amount of time sitting on the dry dock, while God works on us from the inside out, than it is for us to jump into deep waters, ahead of time. It is a contraction, and our expansion will come, in time.

In time.

Part of this dry dock experience can and does apply to relationships. It applies to this subject of Boys, Guys, and Men. Often we're sitting over here on our little dry dock, waiting for Prince Charming to come by on his little speedboat. His white horse speedboat, "Come and pick me up baby and take me away!" The problem with that is that the fast moving speedboat is not a match for the slow moving merchant ship. You need to meet your match.

You are a merchant ship, not some guy's pleasure cruiser or speedboat. It's important to know who you are. You might have all the right curves in all the right places, but you are a merchant ship. We sometimes have to explain this to the opposite sex. We need to make sure it is clear that we know we have been born and built on purpose for God's purpose.

I am a merchant ship. I understand that. I'm not even confused about that anymore. I know who I am. I am a merchant ship, born for capacity. I was talking with a group of very outstanding, gifted, amazing capacious leaders during a particularly stressful season, about the bigness of life. I believe that the only solution to the stress of life, as your life increases on the merchant ship, is that our capacity for our relationship with God must also increase. We can't leave God on the dock as we sail the high waters. We need to understand that the purpose of our capacity is not only for us to be involved in the "industry of ministry", but that we would love Him more. Our relationship with God is the goal, and we must not take our eyes off Him. This merchant ship is big, steely, strong, not pretty. Pretty today, not so pretty in 50 years time, it doesn't matter. This merchant ship is built for life, built to last, built to build. And God has not just given us responsibility, He has also given us gifting. You are gifted. The truth is that God has given you a measure of gifting to go with the responsibility to be a big ship because otherwise we would just say, "I can't cope." God has given us the ability to cope because our DNA is merchant ship. We are built strong to move His purpose from one place to another, and whom we build with will determine how strong we are and how long we will last.

When it comes to this subject of boys, guys, and men, I know that each person reading this book will be in a different place. Some are happily married with kids. Others have been happily married with kids a couple of times. Some are unhappily married. Others have been on our own as a single mom. Others have never been married before. There are so many categories and different scenarios that it would be impossible to address each one specifically. I would like to speak in terms of principle, so that we can grasp what is going to be wisdom in our life, to help build our life. The wise woman builds her life.

And the foolish one tears it down.

Beam by beam.

Ignoring wisdom.

When it comes to choosing a partner for our lives, the first thing we need to do is look at our life and see what kind of person we really are. Do you look fantastic on paper and are you fantastic in person?

build

"A wise woman builds her home, but a foolish woman tears it down with her own hands."

proverbs chapter fourteen verse one
[new living translation]

Are you a woman of integrity, or are you compromised in certain areas of your life? Integrity is simply this: know right and do right. When we know right and do wrong, we are compromised.

When we live lives of integrity, we grow in spiritual maturity and personal security. When we live lives of integrity, we set goals accordingly.

We can chase the guy to get a ring, especially if it looks like a five-carat diamond solitaire! That could be a goal in our life, or we can have a bigger goal. If we are living the speedboat life, we are on a mission to catch the guy as quickly as possible and slow down just long enough to get hitched. However, if we are living the merchant ship life, steadily moving forward with amazing vision and purpose, we might meet a merchant ship man to marry.

We can listen to what the Word of God says. We can listen to what parents, pastors, teachers, leaders and mentors say, or we can ignore everybody. And we can rage against all wise counsel. It's completely up to us. We all know someone who has had a relational train wreck in their life with the opposite sex. We have either been in a situation like this ourselves or someone in our life has.

Life is full of choices.

We need to choose wisely.

We need boundaries.

We need healthy relationships.

Relationships! Who needs them? We all do! Finding and maintaining meaningful relationships is an important factor in building healthy self-esteem into our lives. When our relationships are healthy, it's easy to feel a great sense of achievement and reward.

What is not easy, of course, is building healthy relationships. It takes commitment and work to produce healthy relationships, and the first place we must start is with ourselves. We've often heard it said, or we may have even said it, 'What's a nice girl like her doing with a guy like him?'

A nice girl is with a guy like him perhaps because the nice girl doesn't have a sense of her worth and value. She's living well below the level that she could be living at, and it is more to do with her than the guy. The relationship exists as a result of her poor choice. That is why many nice girls choose guys like him, over and over again. A significant number of people do in fact seem to be attracted to the wrong kind of person for them.

You may feel as though you have a magnet on your forehead that attracts unhealthy relationships. Realizing that fact is a great place to start. When you take personal responsibility and shift the blame from the guy to yourself, you are then empowered to break the cycle of unhealthy relationships and begin to assess how valuable you are and who should and can enter your private world.

When it comes to entering any relationship, no matter what happens, it is important to acknowledge that you have something to do with the relationship. It's called 'personal responsibility.'

UNHEALTHY RELATIONSHIPS

It is easy to get emotional and angry when we see our partner has different values, beliefs or expectations from us. What's important to understand is that there will always be differences in opinions, and how we handle these differences will determine the health of our relationships and how we feel about ourselves. Some of the issues that have a negative impact on relationships are:

- Lack of time spent together
- Lack of communication
- Lack of understanding of views
- Different goals or expectations
- Financial insecurity
- Bringing up children
- Inability to resolve conflict

- Sexual difficulties
- Different cultural backgrounds
- Lack of trust
- Alcohol or drug abuse
- Affairs
- Gambling
- Violence

Everyone who is in a relationship or cares about their relationships may need assistance at some time to help deal with problems and to learn how to improve them. We also need assistance when a relationship breaks down.

There is conflict in all relationships at times, and that is important. Being able to deal with conflict and handle differences in opinion is crucial in building healthy relationships. We cannot eliminate conflict completely, but we can manage it constructively.

CO-DEPENDENCY

People who tend to be naive about relationships also tend to reflect aspects of co-dependency in their relationships. People who are codependent naturally care a lot for people and devote their lives to saving others who are in trouble. They usually try so hard to help and manage someone else's life to save them, but when they fail, their life tends to fall into a crumpled heap of hopelessness because they lose control.

A co-dependent relationship is one where the partners have difficulty being themselves while being in a relationship. In any relationship, people tend to experience the battle between being themselves and being part of a relationship. In a healthy relationship, this can be dealt with openly; as a result, both partners can increasingly feel more secure in the relationship and more intimate as they grow as individuals.

In a co-dependent relationship, these issues are more difficult to deal with. Often they are simply swept under the rug or dealt with in an unhealthy atmosphere of accusations of selfishness, or one partner finds a way to intimidate the other. As a result, there is growing resentment within the relationship. A co-dependent person may otherwise be known as a 'rescuer' or 'martyr' and they are usually attracted to people who need lots of help: such as alcoholics, drug users, sex addicts, the mentally or physically ill and, perhaps most insidiously, selfish, irresponsible or ambitious people who need someone to support them while they look after their own interests.

Unfortunately, people who have co-dependent personalities usually do not see their own problems, nor do they see the need to take responsibility for them. They are only able to recognize their efforts to help others and they wonder why they are not celebrated or rewarded for them. They simply do not see the choices they have made.

How do you know if you might have a co-dependent type personality? Read through the following checklist to see how you rate. Try to be completely honest!

1.   Do you focus solely on wanting others to be happy?

2.   Do you feel responsible for your partner's life?

3.   Do you criticize yourself?

4.   Do you feel excessively guilty and full of shame?

5.   Are you an angry and nagging person?

6.   Do you threaten others?

7.   Do you deny your own problems and need for love?

8.   Do you believe that you can change your partner?

9.   Are you easily depressed?

10.   Do you find it hard to accept what happens to you?

**Freedom from co-dependency is achievable.
Following are some goals:**

1.   You will be able to think and talk about other things besides someone else's problems.

2.   You won't feel the need to change other people's behavior.

3.   You will see your role as an encourager, rather than a rescuer.

4.   You will know when it's time to get out before it's too late.

5.   You will be able to implement tough love, which actually demonstrates the most caring, and has boundaries in place.

Once you understand co-dependency, and begin to accept that you aren't responsible for another person's actions and that you can't control the situation and don't hold the cure for the situation, you can then stop supporting someone else's bad habits and get on with developing a healthy life of your own.

tune in

"Dear friend, listen well to my words. Tune your ears to my voice. Keep my message in plain view at all times. Concentrate, learn it by heart. Those who discover these words will live. They will really live. Body and soul, they're bursting with health."

proverbs chapter four verses twenty to twenty-two
[the message]

chapter eleven

boundaries
healthy
healthy
healthy

boundaries

"Boundaries define us. They define what is me and what is not me. A boundary shows me where I end and someone else begins... Knowing what I am to own and take responsibility for gives me freedom. If I know where my yard begins and ends, I am free to do with it what I like... if I do not 'own' my life, my choices and options become very limited."[1]

Boundaries

by Dr. Henry Cloud and Dr. John Townsend

When you have identified the key issues, and you properly understand your own personal value, it is time to establish some necessary boundaries to protect the health of the relationships in your life. It is vitally important that you don't settle for less than the best for you. That may mean that you have to kiss the harmful and destructive relationships goodbye.

It may be that you will need to detach yourself from the other person and take responsibility for managing only your own life, and in the process, try to be kind to yourself. Detachment or distance from another person does not involve rejecting the actual person, it is simply rejecting the feeling of complete responsibility for them. To become detached from another person requires us to understand who we are. Being able to detach involves having well-defined boundaries.

Sometimes we must make a choice that will require a severing of a relationship, if personal boundaries have been transgressed. Having clear boundaries is essential to a healthy, balanced lifestyle. A boundary is a personal property line that marks those things that we are responsible for. When we establish boundaries, we establish who we are and who we are not, where we want to go and where we do not want to go.

Relational naivety and deception can bring pain, and failure to establish adequate boundaries can leave a person feeling deceived, used, abused and afraid. An absence of boundaries allows us to be lulled into a false sense of security, which in turn, allows us to be led by our feelings and by flattery. This then makes us susceptible to the advances of someone who is setting out to take advantage of us.

That's where sexual boundaries are so important. Our self-esteem affects our attitudes towards sex. Our behavior reflects our self-esteem and our self-esteem reflects in our behavior. A great sex life is experienced when people have identifiable boundaries in place to protect not just their body, but also their soul and spirit.

In their book, 'Boundaries', Cloud and Townsend describe boundaries as "anything that helps to differentiate you from someone else, or that show you where you begin and end".

Problems will arise when we fail to set good boundaries and maintain them and also when we bond to the wrong kind of people and don't bond to the right kind of people. Outside of relationships, boundaries are easy to see. Fences, walls, signs, or hedges are all physical boundaries.

Within relationships, boundaries impact all areas of our lives:

1.   Physical boundaries help us decide who may touch us and under what circumstances. It is your right to say yes or no.

2.   Mental boundaries give us the freedom to have our own thoughts and opinions. It's your right to have freedom of speech.

3.   Emotional boundaries help us to deal with our own emotions, and to deflect the negative and manipulative emotions of others. It's your right to maintain unhindered feelings.

The primary purpose of any wall is for protection. Walls are there to keep vulnerable and valuable things in and harmful things out. However, walls that are built because of fear or negative experiences can isolate and contain you.

Some people learn early on in life that it is unsafe to get too close to others, particularly when someone they love has hurt them. Once this defensive and self-protective belief is instilled, walls are built to protect that belief. The problem is that loneliness and isolation will become an unhealthy by-product.

Other people learn to believe early on in life that in order to be happy, they should have no boundaries at all. The problem with this extremity is that continual heartache and pain will become an unhealthy by-product of this kind of living.

Boundaries assist us to live in balance, providing that the boundaries that we have in place resemble a fence with a gate rather than a brick wall. The fence means that we can see over it and that we can't hide behind it, and the gate enables us to come and go freely and others to come and go as we choose. What you don't want to build into your life is either a brick wall that says, "keep out," or no fence at all that says, "everyone welcome."

CONFLICT MANAGEMENT

When it comes to problems, we need to discover our role so that we can be empowered to make necessary changes. That's when we can either turn the situation around by our actions, perhaps even severing the relationship if appropriate. When we can't see our role in the problem, we lose our power and potentially stay trapped indefinitely.

We've been taught that relationships should be fifty-fifty. In other words, "You do your part, and I'll do mine." I have learned, however that in order to build healthy, strong relationships we need to at least aim to be one hundred–one hundred. The ideal is to aim for a hundred percent, and even if we fall short, there should be enough juice in the relationship tank to compensate. If we only agree to do what is minimal, we can expect disaster. If we agree and try to give a hundred percent, we can expect to flourish relationally.

I believe that every person is responsible for the presence or absence of love. In any relationship, each person is constantly reacting to the other, and we tend to react according to how we are treated. When you are accepted and appreciated by someone, you usually feel loved and automatically accept and appreciate that person in return. But when you are judged or criticized, you become upset, judgmental and critical in return. When we react rather than respond, we are not taking responsibility for our own lives. If you are being mistreated, you are still able to respond constructively without becoming a doormat. In his book 'Love is Never Enough', Dr. Aaron T. Beck analyzes actual dialogue to draw attention to the most common problems experienced by couples, including the power of negative thinking, disillusionment, rigid rules and expectations, and miscommunication.

When looking at the issue of miscommunication in conflict, Dr. Beck says, 'Rather than seeing that there is a misunderstanding, conflicting partners misattribute the problem to the mate's "meanness" or "selfishness". Unaware that they are misreading their spouses, partners incorrectly ascribe base motives to them.'

We can all get it wrong when we try to second-guess each other's motives and feelings, and it's usually just a matter of time before someone gets hurt and upset. We put up walls of protection and resist, attack or withdraw. Then our partner may become upset and do the exact same thing in return and then we become even more upset and react more fiercely, and so the cycle of conflict goes on.

The good news is that to create and maintain this cycle; there must be two people participating. Which means that if you refuse to attack or withdraw or react, then chances are the cycle will be broken, and a fresh start can be made. Once you discover your role in the conflict, you can do something about it. You can end the cycle of conflict and restore the love. Conflict management is the practice of identifying and handling conflict in a sensible, fair and efficient manner through effective communicating, problem solving and negotiating.

We need to live on the right side of 'if '. Instead of saying to ourselves, 'If he apologizes first, then I will apologize,' how about saying, 'If I apologize, then at least I will have peace of heart and mind.' Make the 'if ' relate to your actions, not your partner's. Living on the right side of 'if ' empowers us to live in freedom and to take responsibility for our own lives.

To handle conflict constructively, first you will need to make a decision that you will not attack your partner when you get angry. Decide that when there is a conflict between you, you will aim to resolve it as quickly and as constructively as possible. When conflict arises, and you feel angry with your partner, try to follow these steps:

1.   **Admit that you are angry.**

Try using "I" statements to let your partner know how you are feeling, rather that 'You' statements, which will be heard as an attack and lead the other person to be defensive and therefore make the conflict even worse. However, admitting your anger is different from expressing it. Be strong, but don't shout and swear.

2.   **Ask for time out.**

Resting time out is essential if either you or your partner feels too angry to talk about the problem. Cooling down before discussing the issue is a good idea, but set a limit on it — don't use time out to avoid or ignore the issue indefinitely.

3.   **Check your feelings.**

There is nearly always another feeling underlying anger, like sadness, hurt or disappointment. Let your partner know how you feel. The underlying feeling will usually be a clue to the real issue that you and your partner need to face up to and talk about.

4.   **Listen to your partner's point of view.**

There may be an angle on the situation that you haven't considered.

5.   **Be prepared to acknowledge your part in the problem.**

Being willing to apologize does not mean that you are accepting all the responsibility.

6.   **Ask yourself what you can learn from the conflict.**

This will improve your relationship and lessen the chances of a similar conflict happening again.

7.   **Be prepared to forgive and make up as soon as possible.**

Don't make your partner wait as a punishment. Reunion after conflict can lead to a deepening of closeness and intimacy in a relationship.

Although difficulties in any relationship are normal and many relationships do survive such challenges, healthy relationships are only built with commitment and effort. We can choose to just survive, or we can choose to thrive. It's the difference between existing and living, and it's our choice.

Building Blocks

Acknowledging the existence of an unhealthy relationship is the first step to either restoring or ending it. Taking an inventory of the relationship and identifying the problem areas is the second step, and you may need professional assistance to do this properly.

For some people, the word "relationship" means security, happiness and peace, and for others it simply means shattered dreams and hell on earth.

Relationships come in all shapes and sizes, and every relationship is unique. The variations are seemingly infinite. If life were easy and predictable, here is how the perfect relationship might go:

- You are on your own and feeling all right with yourself.
- You meet someone you would like to get to know better.
- The two of you decide to go out together.
- You both have a really good time on your first date, when you discover what you have in common.
- You go out again and your friendship and relationship grows.
- After going out together several times you both realize you have found someone special.
- You fall in love and continue to go out regularly.
- You decide to get married.
- You plan the wedding together and await the big day.
- You get married.
- You have 2.3 children.
- You live happily ever after.

As you probably realize, life is rarely easy or predictable, so it doesn't always work out according to this list. There are lots of reasons why things don't work out this way very often, and that is because relationships and people can be very different. Not everyone wants the same type of relationship, nor do they want the same type of person. That sounds obvious, but I think we don't really accept it when the person we love is the one who is not agreeing with us. This conflict within a relationship is not exclusive to those people who don't have it all together — it can happen to the 'I've got it all together' people too. When partners view the relationship differently, it can cause endless inner turmoil and will be a key ingredient in an unhealthy relationship.

The good news is that even if you are in the midst of an unhealthy relationship, within every ounce of pain lies a ton of potential. But this requires action and effort. For every bad choice, a good choice needs to be made. The past needs to be left behind and the future needs to be focused on. Life is full of choices. We are all born with a will, and with that will, we make a way for ourselves. We determine our way, the way in which we lead our lives, by our choices.

Choose to live and love.

As the saying goes, 'You need to be cruel to be kind.' Sometimes you just need to be what may seem cruel to that which is hurting you, and kind to yourself. In order to be truly kind to yourself, you need to cut off destructive relationships, even though it seems like the hardest thing you could do.

It is the only way to free yourself up for your future because, at the end of the day, freedom is what you crave and what you need. You deserve to be in a relationship that is totally healthy, totally committed, yet totally free.

For those in destructive relationships, inside the depth of your pain lies the heart of your potential. The potential to rise up and out of the situation you were never created to be in. Whether your pain is your fault or someone else's fault, it's within your power, through your will and your choice, to do something positive about it.

Following are some practical building blocks to help you flourish regardless of your past:

1.   Acknowledge that you are valuable.

2.   Don't receive criticism and abuse and don't give it.

3.   Think carefully about whom you choose to start a relationship with.

4.   Clearly communicate your wishes and respect the wishes of others.

5.   Remember that you have permission to start again.

Many people, unfortunately, go looking for love in all the wrong places. This is all too common a problem. Boy meets girl, boy dumps girl, girl never gets over it!

Life may knock you down to the ground and knock the stuffing out of you, but it's never too late to get back up again. Good people get hurt, and age has nothing to do with it. Relationship breakdown can happen at any time.

If you have made unwise decisions that have landed you in trouble, now is the time to do something positive with your future. Don't drag your pain into your future. The past is the past. You can't change it; no one can. Even if you are a victim of someone else's rotten behavior towards you, you can use it to empower your future. See their behavior as a lesson in what not to do, rise above the pain they inflicted on you by choosing to love and forgive, and this will make you stronger and in charge of your life. No matter what you've been through, remember, you are not a 'has been', you are a 'will be'!

Determining what a healthy relationship should look like is a great place to start. A healthy relationship is based on respect, having fun together, freedom to be yourselves, even when you can have different opinions and interests. Listening to each other is essential. Trust is another important factor, as is an absence of jealousy. Then, of course, there's compromise and the ability to apologize and talk arguments out. Breathing space is also crucial. You don't have to spend all of your spare time together— you can spend time on your own, or with your own friends and family.

For a relationship to be healthy and for you to feel good about yourself, be the one to show goodwill by offering to make it work — don't wait for your partner. You may be pleasantly surprised by how much difference taking the first small step can make. Start with you.

Be supportive and don't make judgments when your partner makes mistakes or does things differently from how you would do them. Ask for help when you cannot cope with the situation. Share the domestic load, offering to do what you like to do most, but being prepared to do whatever it takes for the job to be done. Allow yourself the right to put your feet up and relax and make time specifically for you — have a bath, read, listen to music, spend time with friends.

When you are able to express your feelings honestly and show appreciation to your partner for their contribution; when you listen to others and take responsibility for your own life, then you will begin to see healthy relationships develop and flourish in the future.

If you say, "I love him," ask yourself the reasons why. Is he kind, considerate, caring? Is it real love or infatuation? Is it possible that what you think is love, is anything but? Only real love will last, and it is not an illusion. Look for someone with the qualities that you respect and admire. Being attracted to someone is important initially, but it doesn't mean you will stay attracted to them forever. Wise up and beware of unhealthy relationship traps.

'First-mile love' is primarily about chemistry and feelings, but 'second-mile love' is more about construction, choice and commitment. On that note, I'll leave you with these words from Louis de Bernières's novel Captain Corelli's Mandolin: "Love itself is what is left over when being in love has burned away, and this is both an art and a fortunate accident."[2]

HEALTHY RELATIONSHIP CHECK LIST

1.   You can both manage conflict and differences without despair or threats.

2.   You both protect and nourish the relationship and make it a priority.

3.   You both know how to be responsible for your own needs and also for the care of the relationship.

4.   You both feel 'special' to the other. Arguments or fights do not lead to abuse or threats.

5.   You both communicate wants, needs, feelings and emotional issues with little or no shame.

6.   There is unconditional love.

7.   The relationship feels and is nurturing, comfortable and fun.

8.   You respect each other physically.

9.   Both partners are honest.

10.   There is no abuse — physical, verbal or emotional.

Julie's Story ...

At the age of thirteen, I was so happy to move back to the United States. I had been living overseas for six years and missed the USA. I would be coming back to start high school and much to my surprise the transition from one culture to another was not an easy one to say the least. The 9th grade girls were way more grown up and mature in the ways of life than I was. I didn't wear makeup and had not cared about fashion until now. For the very first time in my life, I understood what it felt like to be ugly. By the time I was in tenth grade I longed for popularity and to have a boyfriend. I had several dates, but nothing that lasted or was real. Throughout the rest of high school, I did just about anything to be loved by a boy or to be popular.

I was lonely...

Straight after high school I landed a great job doing what I'm passionate about. There I met a guy that I thought was very cute and showed interest in me. He had tattoos and a bad boy look and attitude. After six months of dating things started to get serious and he asked me to marry him. We talked to my parents, who counseled us to wait so we could get to know each other. Unfortunately, even though I thought this counsel was wise I didn't listen. I was afraid I would lose this guy and no one would ever ask me to marry them again.

I was afraid of feeling lonely again, so we eloped.

Within less than a month I realized what a big mistake I had made. We had nothing in common! We were completely different in our perspectives and goals. We didn't see eye to eye on anything. My biggest challenge with him was the fact that he didn't like to work, and we were living off just my earnings. Oh yes, and the fact that he was a pathological liar. He would make up stories to make himself sound bigger and better than anyone else. I decided to stay committed and try to make this work. After two years of marriage, I was ready to call it quits.

I was still lonely.

This lonely was worse though. I never knew you could have a partner and still be lonely.

Then something happened.

I became pregnant.

During my pregnancy, we lived in a one-bedroom apartment with my mother-in-law because that is all we could afford with my earnings. My bedroom was the living room, and my bed was two ottomans pushed together. With a large belly, broken shoes and swollen ankles, I worked all day on my feet. I came home from work to find my husband in his underwear in the dark playing video games. No nursery for my child and no bed to call my own.

I was done.

After the birth of my beautiful daughter, I started talking and plotting with my best friend about whether I should get a divorce. In the meantime, I met another guy at work. I was so physically attracted to him that I thought surely someone should have this guy. So I made arrangements to set him up with my best friend. When I introduced them at a large gathering my friend noticed something I had not. She said it was obvious that he was attracted to me.

My new male friend started hanging around my daughter and me all the time. You see, my husband was never around. He was always out and about playing pool, going to concerts and hanging out with his friends. My heart was getting more and more emotionally attached to my new friend. So I decided one day to have a heart-to-heart with my husband and said, "If we don't fix things between us we should get a divorce." His response was, "I think we should get a divorce". I was shocked and I was sad. I remember taking my 9-month-old baby, putting her in a stroller and going for a walk as I cried my heart out. I would later find out that my husband already had a girlfriend and things were truly over with us.

I moved back home with my parents and started my new life with my new boyfriend. My family loved this new guy. He became part of our family and even moved into my parents' home with us. He was funny, hardworking, and he loved my daughter. We grew closer and closer, but there was one thing wrong. He was from the Midwest, and his goal was to move back home within a year. I didn't understand this because I thought he loved my daughter and me. At this point, I would just shove that reality to the side because for the first time I felt love and was loved back. Then the unspeakable happened. I was still in the middle of getting my divorce, and I became pregnant. I told my boyfriend, and he said this could not happen.

He said we should get an abortion.

My self-esteem was so wrapped up in him that I said yes. I faced the abortion with the guilt of already knowing the beautiful reality of pregnancy and childbirth.

I aborted.

I did this pretending like I was so strong (while I was dying inside) that my boyfriend asked me if I had done this before. I had not. I just wanted to be everything I could be for him. So the less drama I created, the better for him. The time came for him to move, and with great sadness and confusion I said my goodbyes, but I was still hopeful. So off he went, what I thought was my love. Two days later he called me ... and he called me every day at that time. After two weeks of his departure he announced to me that he missed me and my daughter so much that he was coming back to marry me and start a life together. I was exhilarated, to say the least.

It was a very romantic long distance relationship. Our plan was that in four months I would fly to his hometown to attend his brother's wedding then we would drive back down to Florida to start our lives together. In the meantime, my grandfather got very ill. My grandfather was the one who had taught me about Jesus and had taken me as a child to church every Sunday. He soon passed away and his death really shook my world. I started thinking about God again. I thought about what eternity looked like for me and what exactly my purpose was here on earth. During this time I turned to my boyfriend for comfort only to suddenly feel a weird kind of distance. I knew something was wrong in our relationship but didn't know what. He was just not the same and very, very cold towards me.

On my way to the Midwest for the wedding, I was hopeful but terrified. Deep down in my heart I knew there was something truly wrong. When I saw him at the airport, my stomach sank. It was an awkward encounter. I went to his home and met all his family. They were very lovely and very nice to me. Among the wedding activities, my boyfriend and I decided to spend some alone time together to try and reacquaint ourselves with each other. Finally, the truth came out. My boyfriend was scared of making a commitment to my daughter and me. He said he was scared to get married and he was scared that he would not love me forever.

I became angry, sad and confused.

I didn't know what to do.

On the day of the wedding, since my boyfriend was part of the bridal party, I was given a seat at the "out-of- town-ers" table. Next to me sat a very jolly, quirky California guy. He was very friendly with me, and we spent the entire wedding together. He gave me his business card and said if my boyfriend and I ever wanted to come to California for vacation, to give him a call. The day after the wedding was the day my boyfriend and I were to drive back down to my home. It was a terrible, long two-day trip home. At this point, I was angry at him for making me think we were to get married, and now he changed his mind? I didn't understand. On our arrival home, I was fully enraged and could not stop crying. My boyfriend explained to my parents that he was not sure if he loved me or wanted to marry me. I walked out of my room to hear my mother telling him that he needed to make up his mind. He needed to decide if I was the one or not. If I were not the one then he should leave now. He got up walked out the door, got in his car and I never saw him again.

This next season in my life was a very painful one. I lost all desire to live. I couldn't even be a proper mother to my daughter. I didn't know who I was or why I existed. I was angry at God. I didn't understand that if God loved me so much why He would not give me the one thing that I wanted. One afternoon I was going off in one of my angry spews at God while I was speaking to my dad, when suddenly he slipped me a business card for a Christian therapist. What? ...Oh well, I had nothing to lose. So I called Simon, my new therapist. Through Simon's wise counseling, the healing process started in my heart, and I started to feel grace, for the first time.

Grace was new to me.

I didn't even know what it meant.

I started to pray and started going back to church. One evening at church they were asking for people to come to the front if they wanted a relationship with God. I heard this question a dozen times when I was a child. But this time my heart was pumping fast, and I felt a sudden urge to go forward. So I went. The couple that was waiting there to pray for me asked me what I wanted. I said I wanted God in my life again, but I was afraid. The gentleman said, "It's ok. You're afraid of the unknown." He started to pray for me, and as he prayed for healing, I felt a sudden feeling of extreme joy. I just wanted to smile and laugh. I had never felt this happy in my entire life.

After this encounter with God, I was never the same. I was happy and I wanted to do the things I had dreamed of. I dreamed of things that I felt God had put in my heart. My grandfather, an immigrant from Europe, had always talked about moving to California. I wanted to see why he loved California so much. I kept thinking of the California guy I had met at the wedding. I kept his business card so I decided to call him and ask him if he could show me California. To my surprise, when I called him he said "Yes!" So off I went on my California vacation.

Wow! I fell in love with California. My friend Hugo showed me all around. The glitz, the glam, the fashion, the lifestyle. That is where I belonged. My week in California came to an end. Hugo took me to the airport, and as I was getting ready to board, he handed me a note. It was a love letter where Hugo confessed his feelings for me. As I read the letter I was flattered but I knew deep down inside that I didn't have the same feelings. I was not physically attracted to him. Nevertheless, I knew I had to move to California, so I kept in contact with Hugo.

In the months to come I made preparations to move to California. I sent my resume out to several companies hoping to land a dream job. I talked to my parents about it, and they gave me their blessings. They were happy to send me. Within a week, I got a call back from the store. They wanted to interview me. I flew to California for an interview and landed the job. So I gathered my stuff and my daughter and moved to California. Hugo was very generous and helped me through the process. Since I didn't really know anyone, I spent most of my time with Hugo and his family.

Even though I knew that living in California was the right thing to do, being away from my family was hard. For the first month, I cried all the way to work. I hated leaving my daughter in childcare. My daughter had always stayed with my mom or grandmother. I missed family. The one thing that kept me going was God. I knew he had a purpose for me here. The other person that encouraged me was Hugo's stepmother Jenny. She was loving, fun, and full of laughter. Holidays with her were unlike anything I had ever experienced before. I loved Jenny as my adoptive mother. She made her home our home. My daughter also loved her as a grandmother. She was our new family in California.

Life was good except for one thing... HUGO.

I wasn't attracted to him, and I knew the only reason he would come to church is because of me and not because of Jesus. Just like me pretending in my head that I loved him, Hugo was pretending to love Jesus. Here I was a Christian, still not freed from loneliness. If I broke up with him that meant I would break up with his stepmother Jenny, and I would not have a family. So what was my solution? I asked him to marry me. Of course he said yes. Time passed, and guilt set in on my decision. As a daughter of God, I was a hypocrite and made decisions based on feelings, and I wasn't thinking about my daughter. I had already birthed her into a broken home, and now I was putting her through yet another situation where she would find separation and divorce again.

Based on my beliefs, I was not having sex with Hugo because that is what my Bible says. Honestly it was easy to follow that conviction since I was not physically attracted to him. I also felt tremendous guilt. I was living a lie. I was lying to my God, my daughter, Hugo, Jenny and myself. I couldn't bear it. One day oddly enough Jenny gave me a book called "What Stupid Women Do To Mess Up Their Lives." I read it and was completely convicted to change my life. I broke up with Hugo.

The difference between conviction and guilt is the following:

Guilt keeps repeating itself.

Conviction from the Holy Spirit makes a change.

Now here is the twist – when I decided to break up with Hugo is when he told me that he had gotten another girl pregnant. So here I was, on my own with my daughter. Once again round 3 of division, separation and divorce.

This time without family.

Here I was a new person. I was convinced that I and God could do this on our own. I would work hard, raise up my daughter in the ways of God and move forward. What I didn't know is that I had not dealt with loneliness. The other thing I didn't know was that doing things alone was not what God intended. Not to mention that I did not have the support group of the church and I lacked the wisdom of God's Word. I heard God's Word every Sunday in church, but I didn't read the Bible every day. Five years passed and here I was a single mom doing it on my own. I hated the financial struggle and the status struggle and not knowing who I was.

Then along came Peter. He was hard working, stable, owned a beautiful home, and called himself a Christian. I wasn't physically attracted to him, but I thought that since he went to church I could grow to love him. He had a son, and I thought we could blend families. Here is what was wrong with this relationship: being a Christian is more than just going to church on Sunday. We didn't know what it was to take the Bible for truth and apply it to our everyday life. We didn't know what it meant to be in community with believers. So here I was, a Christian, living in the same house as my fiancé, trying to make things work. No Bible, no community, no wisdom. No spiritual connection. We attended pre-marital classes at my request. He hated it and all I saw were red flags. Things got so unsecured around our home that I couldn't even go out with my friends without getting the third degree. I felt trapped, not to mention all that came with blending families. On the weeks that his son was home, my daughter and I felt like second best. As an example, when it was just us I could sit in the front seat of the car. When his son was home, I sat in the back. That was the norm. This is where for the first time I felt completely disconnected from my daughter.

I went to a local conference with my friend. I had to lie about going there because my fiancé didn't like me hanging out with my Christian friend. At the conference I felt totally convicted. Again, conviction is not guilt but making a change in your life. I knew that I had to move out of my fiancé's home and trust God. I knew that it was time to finish things. The first person I told was my daughter, who was probably too young to hear this. She was afraid. For the first time in my life I realized that she trusted men for security more than she did God. She was following in my footsteps.

For the first time in my life I took steps, trusting God. I trusted that

He would provide. I trusted that he would protect. I trusted that he would fill the gap for my fatherless child, and I trusted that He would help me not to feel alone. I moved out and made Matthew 6:33-34 my motto. To seek God in everything I do, and He will give me everything I need.

So nine years have passed and this where I am. My daughter and I are planted in a home church that has radically changed our lives. We are definitely living for a cause bigger than ourselves. We have a huge church family that fills our home and lives.

I have learned how to be healthy without needing a man to fill any void in my life.

I have learned to establish healthy boundaries for myself and my daughter.

I am now married to the man of my dreams.

My husband loves God, loves me, and loves my daughter. Life and love might have come late for me, but let's just say that if I have missed out on anything, God has definitely made up for it now. I now know what it feels like to be connected spiritually, emotionally and physically to a man.

Love is spectacular, and God is grand.

God is grand!

10 KEYS TO FREEDOM FROM UNHEALTHY RELATIONSHIPS

1.   Forgive everyone who's hurt you in a relationship. That may take time, but commitment to the process will set you free.

2.   Throw away things that remind you of pain in your past relationships.

3.   Don't call or harass a former partner, as it will only damage your self-esteem even further.

4.   See yourself as valuable and choose your relationships accordingly — the Prince/Princess is so much better than the Beast.

5.   Don't make the same mistake twice — solving a problem fixes a problem, not repeating it.

6.   Walk away from an abusive relationship and get help from family or friends.

7.   Lift your future standards higher than your past experience. Just because you have had ogres in the past, doesn't mean that is all you deserve to have.

8.   Don't replace one dependency for another, such as relationships for drugs or alcohol.

9.   Don't allow yourself to be pressured into sex.

10.   Dare to believe that your future is very bright!

respect

"The beginning of love is to let those we love be perfectly themselves, and not to twist them to fit our own image. Otherwise we love only the reflection of ourselves we find in them."[3]

Thomas Merton

chapter twelve

the lean of faith
lean
lean
lean

Before we allow ourselves to fall in love with someone who could possibly be the wrong person for us, it's important to learn how to "lean". The lean of faith is an essential part of getting to know each other. It involves risk of rejection, but it is a healthy way to explore potential without falling down flat.

1.   **When to lean.**
     [timing]

     Timing is important. If you start dating too early, you have a long and possibly problematic road ahead. On the other hand, if you start dating too late in life, you may never feel ready to start. As long as you are mature enough to handle a relationship, and you understand that the purpose of dating is to find your future partner, and then begin but go slow.

2.   **Where to lean.**
     [setting]

     When you are getting to know someone, it's important to do so in different settings. Candle-lit dinners aren't our every day real life, so be sure to also do simple things like spending time together with each other's families. Also, go on outings with other friends. Be sure to mix with your single friends as well as couples. This will help keep you both emotionally and relationally healthy while you are getting to know each other.

3.   **How to lean.**
     [boundaries]

     Lean lovingly, lean respectfully, lean intentionally, lean knowingly, lean advisedly, but lean – don't fall. Leaning means you are showing your intention, but you can straighten back up again if the feelings aren't reciprocated. Leaning is risky but it is essential. Lean, but be careful not to fall too soon.

4.   **Who to lean towards.**
[selection]

Please refer to Chapter 10 This chapter [written by my husband Jonathan] will help you build a healthy relationship by understanding the power of a three-fold cord that is not easily broken. The three components are as follows:

-    **Chemistry**
     [passion]
-    **Call**
     [purpose]
-    **Construction**
     [plan]

5.   **Why lean not fall.**
[wisdom]

Some women are addicted to love. It is too easy to allow your feelings to take the lead when we should be exercising wisdom instead. Many a relationship has started because of physical attraction but has ended because of lack of any real substance. There is a lot to be said for slowly but surely being the way to win a race. The competition is not between you and other women; it is all about you completing your race in your lane in life. Don't feel pressured into rushing into a relationship because of your age or stage. Remember, marry in haste, regret at your leisure.

Sydney's Story ...

It was the spring of 1968 in my mom's senior year of high school when she found out she was pregnant with me. In those days, the girls in her same situation were going to Mexico to have abortions. She was brave and said she never had to think twice about it; she always wanted me. She got to walk with her class and graduated one week before having me. Choosing to keep me was the first of many brave decisions made out of love for me even if life didn't bring her some of the outcomes she was hoping for.

My mom and dad truly loved each other and wanted to make us a family and decided to marry even though they were so young. The pressures however from never really being accepted by my grandparents became too much and after three years they went separate ways. They always remained friends and I never heard my mom say one bad thing about my dad. However, my dad never came around much. I later realized that his rejection actually became my rejection. This showed me that when you're a boy you will leave and not stay committed to the relationships in your life that are suppose to mean something to you. I was left and felt abandoned, unloved and unwanted by the first important man in my life.

In the start of my first grade year, I'll never forget how lucky I felt because I had the best teacher! I was having the greatest year ever and was actually doing so well in school that I got promoted from first to third grade. My teacher lived in the same area as I lived, and I carpooled with her to and from school everyday. Sometimes I would even go home with her for extra activities. As great as school was going it didn't really line up with what was going on at home. My mom had remarried out of the pressures of feeling the need to provide for us, she later told me.

I was never comfortable around this guy and our home felt violated as he left porn magazines lying around everywhere. I hated going to bed at night because I could never, for the life of me, understand why they had to have sex in the same bed with me in it. Every night I silently screamed inside, "Stop it!" At this very young age I saw that when a guy isn't a respecter of physical boundaries, you are made to feel devalued, confused and robbed of your innocence.

For the next several years, my mom really struggled being on her own and she dealt with addiction. I lived with my grandparents and my mom moved away. My grandpa took me to see her on the weekends but would only leave me if she were sober. They were pretty dark years and my mom even landed herself in jail. She begged my grandma not to bring me to see her for a visit, but my grandma brought me anyway. Looking back now my mom was probably right; jail isn't a place a young girl should be visiting her mother. It was just as hard on my mom as she didn't want me to have memories of her like that.

I spent my next year with Sean Cassidy and reading the 'Hardy Boys' and listening to the Bee Gees, Elvis Presley, and Fleetwood Mac albums. My best friend was my Siamese cat, and I loved Charlie's Angels, as all the girls my age did at that time. Mom got back on her feet and remarried again. I was still doing well academically even though things at home were again not good.

Chaos would interrupt the calm within the house, and it would trigger a new routine of fight-or-flight response to survive.

This time, mom had married an angry guy who would beat her. I would keep a dime in my shoe because as soon as things started to turn violent I needed to run across the street to a pay phone to call for help from my grandpa to come. I had become a protector of my mother, when in fact parents are supposed to be protectors of their children. Again robbing me of my childhood and exposing me to things a child should not have to go through.

One night this guy, my new step-father, masterminded a plan that nearly killed my mom. That showed me that in marriage people can be mean and physically harm you and he showed me what it was to live in fear.

Going into my junior high years, my mom got a good job, and we moved out from living with my grandparents. It was a bitter sweet time for me because I left my cousin who was like a sister to me and also the home I'd known most at a very pivotal time in my life. I became a little rebellious like most kids do at that age.

This season is full of memories of a guy who started showing up in the early mornings before my mom would have to go to work. The bedroom noises would wake me up, and I became disheartened at the decisions that were being made with no consideration of me once again.

My poor mom.

Poor me.

To make matters worse, I soon found out the guy was married and had a step-child. He ended up leaving them for us. I, in no way, accepted him, respected him or wanted to have anything to do with him. But my mom loved him and they got married and now he was able to make my rules and had all say so over me. Mom did not want to lose him. She wasn't willing to lose him to save her relationship with me.

I was preparing to start high school and things at home were actually going pretty well. My 'new dad' asked if he could adopt me so we could all have the same last name. This was something that I had never had before and made me feel like I would be a part of a real family. Since I was starting a new school, we decided to start me off with his last name so when the legal paperwork came through we didn't have to change it. That wasn't such a good idea because by my sophomore year, he left us for another family, just the same way he came to us.

This guy showed that marriage is not sacred, is expendable, and not worth fighting for. By my senior year in high school my mom reconnected with a great friend from high school and once again remarried. This time she married a man that had always loved her and had waited many, many years for her. He had been there for her when I was a toddler and held us both in his heart all the years. He was amazing, and it was the best years of our lives.

After I had graduated from high school, I had resorted to thinking that I was not going to be getting married, and I didn't need to have a marriage as a part of my future. I was going to be independent after growing up with my mom not being very successful with her five marriages.

I had also found myself to be in a place where I had made some unwise choices with my relationships and was living a reckless life worse than anybody even knew. I was being attracted to the same types of negative, "bad-boy" guys that my mom had chosen and would not add anything of value to my future. I was living a double life of a party girl addicted to cocaine at nights and pre-med student girl in the days.

I woke up one day and knew I had to make a change because if I didn't my lifestyle would kill me! I made a decision to fight for my future, go back home, leave the unhealthy relationships I was connected to and got off drugs in time to get accepted to med school.

Staying busy to stay sober, I worked two jobs waiting until the next term started for new students at school. I had sworn off all boys and focused on staying on track. It's usually in these seasons when you're least expecting that the one special man will be sent just in the right time! Regardless of what my plans were for a relationship, I had met a man who believed in me, supported me, and loved me for me and got married. When I was pronounced "Mrs...", I'll never forget how it felt to finally have a name with someone who said we would be together forever!

About five years into my marriage an old friend stopped by to see me at a time when I was feeling very vulnerable about my weight that I had gained after my second baby. She offered me a quick fix, and I took the bait thinking I could do it just once or twice and drop a little weight and that would be it. My very first high was the beginning of a whole year nightmare that I found myself in and didn't know how to get out. I didn't know that no matter how long you have been clean, if you ever go back you start right at the same level where you left off. I was so embarrassed and ashamed I didn't know how to go to my loving husband who has loved me unconditionally and admit my problem. I kept thinking each day that this will be the day I stop just like I always had the times before. What I had been modeled growing up was if things aren't good then the outcomes aren't good either. I was terrified if I told my husband then I would end up alone and in a place that was too familiar, and I didn't want to end up there.

At this same time in April 1996, I got the dreaded phone call that my dearest step-dad, who my son is named after, had committed suicide. I was devastated.

The timing didn't help with me being able to deal with the addiction that was now taking over my life.

I finally came to the end of myself, and I took the risk to come clean with my husband. We felt my only option was to go into rehab and deal with the problem I couldn't kick on my own. The program didn't help me deal with what got me there in the first place, and that was my low self-esteem. Therefore, I gained more weight than I could mentally deal with while in the program and on my first day out, my first call was to my dealer and I relapsed. Having no skills for success, I failed. Giving my husband no other choice but tough love, he took the kids and started to file for a legal separation. My biggest fear became my reality, and I was left all alone.

My relapse was the reality I needed to give me a real wake up call, and I decided I wasn't going to let my past define my future. I leaned on the strength of God and rededicated my life, desperately needing a

Savior to save me from the mess I had made of my life. I worked to build a trust again between me and my husband because he was always the one man who loved unconditionally, stayed committed, and never gave up on me. I was given a second chance, and I didn't take anything for granted. With hard work, we stuck together to rebuild our marriage and our commitment to each other and family has kept us 23 years now still going strong! We have kept Jesus in the center of our lives, and our relationship, and we have a common purpose that keeps us spiritually strong and focused in Him.

EIGHT KEYS TO CHANGE

1.   Be committed to discipline.

I realized that setting boundaries for my children was because I loved them, and I wanted what was best for them. I wish someone had put that hedge of protection around me and set boundaries from a place of discipline. Boundaries mean love in my dictionary. Being committed to discipline in marriage was what kept me focused on the bigger picture of working for something that may not have been modeled well to me growing up. I choose now to be a good wife and good example to my children.

2.   Redefine your parenting!

Let your children see how you work hard and play hard. Life is not one endless list of chores to be crossed off the list! Life is a celebration to be cherished in every stage. Stay alert to the privilege of being a parent, of being in their limitless company, of being able to teach them through your continuous, steady example of love, fairness, kindness and generosity in humility. Believe the best in them and show them how wonderful they are, and they will be!

3.   Be grateful.

Choose to be in an attitude of being grateful, and you will look at life as a precious gift. Do for others because you want to, not because they will be thankful. Whatever you do, do it with love and a pure heart and because you want to do the right thing at the right time for the right reasons because it's a good thing to do. This is all coming from a place of not wanting to take anything or anyone for granted because you know how truly blessed you are! I would rather be loved than thanked – no one can ever let you down when you have no expectation of being anything more than loved!

4.   Don't be a runner!

Keep doing what you're doing and don't runaway. Stay diligent to being a student of wisdom until you can become a teacher. Always look to come alongside someone else to give them a hand up. And then find something new again to learn and add to your life and sow for future generations to enjoy. Never stop learning, never give up, and never give in.

5.   Grow up!

Our personal happiness is up to us. You cannot put unfair expectations on others to make you happy or to understand what you are feeling all the time. Be confident enough in yourself to listen and hear your own voice. Take personal responsibility to do what only you can do to be happy, whole and free. Keep yourself in a place of peace with everyone and yourself.

6.   Don't save the best for last!

What we do with our 'NOW' moments affects what comes later. You are a party, and your presence is a place of strength and inspiration to people you spend time with. Make memories every chance you get and see it as a gift you are giving away to everyone you value in your life. Be intentional in making plans even when it may require a little extra work. The work always pays off in the end when you capture the unrepeatable, fleeting 'now' moments. The best is always what we have today!

7.   Choose to stand up!

Be resilient! Through the habit of making wise choices when faced with obstacles, we build our strength of character. It is where you find the strength, the innermost desire to drive you to stand up when everything else in you is telling you to sit down. Don't let anything keep you from finishing strong. People will be waiting to see you fail. Stay persistent to why you started in the first place, see yourself in the end with the highest heels on and standing tall!

8.   Choose forgiveness.

It is in the hard times, not the easy ones that we learn and gain strength. In order to live a great life of love and happiness promised to all of us, choose to forgive and to be unoffended at all costs. Don't fall trap to the wounds and hurts that offense may cause in your life but instead do whatever it takes to walk in love and forgiveness for a purpose-filled life in freedom!

courage

"You don't develop courage by being happy in your relationships everyday. You develop it by surviving difficult times and challenging adversity."[1]

Epicurus

chapter thirteen

Hey little girl

grow up

grow up

grow up

Our identity is formed when we are children. When our childhood is healthy, we have the opportunity to stay emotionally healthy. For those whose childhood has been robbed of its innocence, healing needs to happen in order to bring health into that person's life. This can happen during childhood, or left not dealt with; this will eventually need to be faced, for anyone hoping for a healthy relationship in the future.

Transitioning from childhood to adolescence is difficult enough but if there has been any form of emotional, physical or sexual abuse involved, this transition can be traumatic.

The good news is that healing and health are possible.

It's easy for us to judge behavior without understanding why people behave the way the do.

Immaturity

Insecurity

Bullying

Addictions

Acting out.

The problem of abuse is widespread. What we know is that since statistics have been kept by welfare departments, the number of children reported and confirmed as having been abused continues to increase.

This may be due to a number of factors including growing community awareness, professional education, media reports and TV programs, legal requirements and a change in society's attitude towards breaking the silence surrounding family violence.

While a similar percentage of boys and girls were abused by strangers, percentages varied when comparing abuse at the hands of a family member or a known person. 40 percent of boys were assaulted by a family member and 56 percent by a known person, while the percentages for girls is reversed — 56 percent were assaulted by a family member and 40 percent by a known person.

Because an allegation of child sexual abuse provokes such strong emotions, and the consequences to both the family and the alleged offender are so serious, it can sometimes be difficult ensuring that a balanced appraisal is made. That is also why it is imperative to seek professional help if you, a friend or a family member has been sexually assaulted.

There is evidence that the immediate effects of severe abuse (physical or sexual) can be catastrophic for children, resulting in mental retardation, brain damage or death. The long-term consequences can also be devastating, leaving physical and emotional scars which result in psychiatric illness, an inability to form meaningful relationships and unusual aggressiveness, which may be turned inward (youth suicide has doubled in the last twenty years) or outward as assault behavior, with the victims repeating the abuse inflicted upon them.

In a study of sexual offenders, it was found that nearly half of them had been child victims of abuse. Not all people who have been abused go on to become abusers, however, many who abuse have been abused themselves. The same pattern is observed in school bullies. Bullies have typically been bullied at some stage, yet not all bully victims go on to become bullies themselves. Parental or self-blame is one catalyst as to why victims sometimes become offenders.

While it is true that severe abuse in childhood can have severe consequences, it is important to acknowledge that an end can be brought to this cycle of abuse. If children feel blamed for their abuse, they are more likely to become abusers. However, if the blame is taken from them by a loving adult who instead communicated understanding, protection, and acceptance they are less likely to become abusers themselves.

Generally speaking, evidence suggests that abusive parents have difficulty controlling their impulses, low self-esteem, a poor capacity for empathy and are socially isolated. Environmental factors such as poverty, poor housing and chronic illness are not sufficient causes, but such stresses combined with poor parenting skills and a sense of having little control over one's life are all contributing factors.

Physical abuse or domestic violence is another major issue.

Domestic violence can be defined as a pattern of behavior in any relationship that is used to gain or maintain power and control over an intimate partner. Domestic violence is abuse. Abuse is physical, sexual, emotional, economic or psychological actions or threats of actions that influence another person. This includes any behaviors that frighten, intimidate, terrorize, manipulate, hurt, humiliate, blame, injure or wound someone.

Domestic violence can happen to anyone of any race, age, sexual orientation, religion or gender. It can happen to couples who are married, living together or who are dating. Domestic violence affects people of all socioeconomic backgrounds and education levels.

The statistics are both alarming and tragic:

- One in every four women will experience domestic violence in her lifetime.
- An estimated 1.3 million women are victims of physical assault by an intimate partner each year.
- 85% of domestic violence victims are women.
- Females who are 20-24 years of age are at the greatest risk of non-fatal intimate partner violence.
- Domestic violence is the leading cause of injury to women.
- Most cases of domestic violence are never reported to the police.

Although these statistics are useful, it is widely believed that the incidence of human trafficking and domestic violence is greater than what is currently being reported, as many victims feel unable to speak out. These inaccurate statistics exist because many victims feel unable to speak out. The pressures of negative community attitudes towards them and feelings of shame and fear of retribution from the perpetrator, contribute to low levels of disclosure of violence and other forms of abuse as well.

Also, because domestic violence often occurs in the privacy of the home, there are few outside witnesses. Surveys often require fluency in English, which means that the experience of people from non-English speaking backgrounds may not be adequately represented.

Abuse is abuse.

Verbal.

Emotional.

Physical.

Sexual.

Abuse is abuse.

Lauren's Story ...

I was born to a loving father and mother. I have a sister two years older than me. When I was three years old, we moved into my grandparents' house while my parents were working on finding our little family a new place to call home. It was under my grandparents' roof that my grandfather began to abuse me sexually. My parents weren't aware that they should even be cautious of this. I don't recall much of what happened, but my mother told me that I walked up to her as a three-year-old and told her what my grandfather was doing. We moved out that instant and lived in the garage of a family friend until we found a place live. Unfortunately, even though that situation ended, sexual abuse reoccurred in my life around the ages six to eight.

I went to a small private school until I was in the 5th grade, where I had become popular among my classmates. I was taller than all the boys in my class and used to arm wrestle them. I felt awkward inside, but no one at school would tease me cause I was the tallest, and I was funny. I used to bully some of the younger girls because I was jealous of their lighthearted girly-ness. Even at that young of an age I could recognize that I felt something had been taken from me. I didn't feel as innocent and sweet as they seemed. When I was alone, I felt uncomfortable in my skin. Even getting dressed I would feel dirty and had a deep sense of shame in myself. By the time I was ten years old I had two younger brothers, and it was time for our family of six to move from a two-bedroom apartment to a bigger house. With this move came not only a new neighborhood, but also a new school, and new friends.

When my public school began I quickly learned that I had no sense of fashion, but I quickly made friends because although I felt awkward, I was still funny. I was teased by the boy I had a crush on because of my overbite and the retainers I used to have to wear. That added to my insecurity and the pain that I had felt from the opposite sex. I wanted to be pretty. I wanted to be liked. I started forming friendships with bossy girls who were pretty and popular because I wanted to have the confidence they had, but I quickly realized these girls were bullying me. They were entertained by my need to have their acceptance. I stopped being friends with them and reverted back to silly behavior and making people laugh. Crushes never turned into boyfriends because I was so awkward with the boys I liked.

While in 7th grade, my aunt committed suicide. This affected me greatly because I had been constantly told by family members that I was just like her. She had been my favorite aunt. She would play theatrical games with my siblings and me, and she sang beautifully. A few years before she died she had made many unhealthy choices for her life, some that lead me to not see her for years at a time. I had known that she was struggling with depression among other things, but I wasn't prepared for what she did. I later learned that she had been sexually abused for years. It had been a compliment to be compared to her in the past, but now it seemed like a curse that I would end up like her. Fear and insecurity were seeping deeper and deeper into the layers of my heart and mind.

At home, my younger brothers had taken it upon themselves to remind me of my awkward pre-teen figure and started calling me names. My older sister was athletic and in good shape so we looked very different. She too would join in the name calling so I would tell on them, making me the ugly duckling and the tattletale.

As a 14-year-old, the summer before my freshman year, I went on a three-day vacation with one of my aunts and uncle to help babysit their toddler. A friend of my uncle came too, and he immediately made me feel uncomfortable. He showed me inappropriate attention, and I would catch him staring at me. He tried to give me beer and get me to ride with him in his truck to the next place we were going. I was so terrified by him that I refused, much to the embarrassment of my aunt, who scolded me for "being rude". I had already felt uncomfortable around most older men, but this added to my wariness of men in general.

While in high school I realized that I loved the performing arts: singing, dancing, and drama. I was good at them. I learned that I could become a chameleon. This I used greatly to my advantage in not only making friends but in getting guys to like me. All I had to do was figure out the kind of girls they liked, and act like that! This worked well for me until I got my first serious boyfriend. I was 15, and he was 18 and went to a different school. He was popular and a baseball player. I had acted like the kind of girls he liked. I had stopped being really funny and started to let him be the center of attention. I bought cuter, tighter clothes. I acted like I was a confident girl, comfortable in my own skin.

The first time we ever went out somewhere as boyfriend and girlfriend, he pulled the car over, and I realized that he wanted more from me physically than I was comfortable with. I didn't speak up. I wanted to be cool. I thought that this is just what all guys want from me. I felt that I was worthless outside of physical affection, so I allowed him to push my boundaries further and further. We were together for about six months but when I refused to sleep with him (and when he realized it really wasn't going to happen) he broke up with me. I had pretended to be ok with what was happening in our relationship for the most part, but sleeping with him, with anyone, terrified me. Some girls that are sexually abused become very promiscuous; some girls shut down. I shut down. I had let him push me past what I was comfortable with and had given him my heart as well. I thought I loved him. He told me he loved me. And then he dropped me. I felt worthless. I felt used and worthless. My response was hostility.

As I entered my junior year of high school every "cool" guy I saw put me on edge. They were a constant reminder of my rejection, of how unlovable and awkward I was. I struggled with depression for the next three years. I didn't know who I was, and I didn't like anything I saw in myself. My parents were there for me but going through a lot personally themselves, and I was insistent on keeping everything to myself. My Dad was a loving and kind man, but unfortunately, I felt uncomfortable around him, simply because he was an older man.

By the time I was 19, I was a ticking time bomb of rejection, insecurity, identity confusion, with deep wells of pain. I lived with major emotional wounds that I had just slapped a Band-Aid over and tried to keep going. I had frequented therapy and even had a prescription for my depression. I had multiple meltdowns where I wanted to kill myself, but I didn't want to hurt my family. I coped by staying out with friends until 4am and sleeping until 2 or 3pm. I would be whoever I wanted to be. I would meet guys and make out with them. This escape quickly became an addiction. I needed to be someone else, and I needed someone's arms around me.

During my teenage years, I used to dream of being married by the age of 20. Well, 20 came and went, and I found myself in one dramatic short-term relationship followed by another. I was terrified of "cool" guys so I started to pick "head-cases", artists, or musicians. They were so obsessed with themselves that they really didn't make any effort to know me. I didn't fear rejection from them since they didn't ever see the real me. I would throw myself into their troubles, art, or lives to escape my own. I let them identify me. I would never let them get too close, and I would always, always push them away eventually. I had so much unresolved pain that I was repeating unhealthy behavior in relationships. When they would break down it just re-affirmed the broken view I had of myself. I strongly believed that I wasn't good enough. I needed peoples' approval, affection, and attention to make me feel valuable. For so long I had avoided facing myself, sometimes because I didn't want to deal with the pain, and sometimes because life was coming at me so fast I didn't have time to process what was actually happening inside me.

The best thing that could have ever happened to me, happened to me in my 20's, and it actually happened to me twice. It was the process of the deconstruction and reconstruction of my life. On two separate occasions I was able to leave the environment I was in (that I had made unhealthy), and go somewhere healthy to renew my mind and to face the issues inside myself. Both places were full of good counsel, truth, and unconditional love. I cannot express what both of those very different places did for me. And although healing was a process, the greatest freedom I have found from all of my confusion and pain has come from facing it, head on. Freedom came from being willing to go back to the painful places in my heart and mind, even though some of it I couldn't remember. I became willing to take the places where "unlovable" and "worthless" had branded me and to let those words be replaced by "absolutely lovable" and "absolutely valuable."

Absolutely lovable.

Absolutely valuable.

I learned to let forgiveness soften what had become hardened in me. I read a lot of counseling books, I prayed A LOT, I accepted that I wasn't perfect, and I embraced God's love and grace. I had to choose to let my life be deconstructed so that it could be properly reconstructed.

I emerged from my 20's unmarried but whole, for the first time in my life. Although many issues didn't disappear with the flicking of a light switch, I now see my 20's like a time where a dimmer was moved steadily from darkness through haze to light. I now live in the light. I have more clarity about my value, worth, and purpose than I ever have before. And now I'm glad I didn't get married in my 20's; I would have put that poor guy through hell. I was a mess, and I would have brought him into my mess.

Now that I'm in my 30's I look back and can see that my life had a lot of great boys, guys, and men in it who treated me well and valued me, who at times warned me about my bad choice in boyfriends, who drove me home when I was having a meltdown and were patient and kind to me. I now have a great relationship with my dad, and I've been able to see and appreciate how he always cherished and valued me. My siblings are my best friends now, and we have all apologized to each other for hurtful things we said and did growing up.

Now that I have dealt with my past, what I have gained is a choice. I now have a clearer mind when I am confronted with what sometimes seems second nature: those old feelings of being worthless, unlovable or rejected. When I am confronted with the ugliness of these feelings that used to define me I GET TO CHOOSE to replace them with the truth. No one can choose for me, I have to choose. I'm no longer confused as to what relationships are healthy or unhealthy. I can identify and choose healthy relationships. I am no longer unwilling to speak up. I choose not to compromise what I think and feel or what I'm comfortable with for fear that I'll lose the relationship. I am worth being heard and being respected. And thankfully, I'm not hostile towards men anymore. My future is bright, not because I am perfect or men are perfect, but because I have learned how to value myself as well as others.

I have learned that men cannot fix me, and that is not what relationships with people are for. I have learned that I am responsible for keeping myself healthy and happy. And with a happy and healthy heart, I can love people rightly.

10 KEYS TO FREEDOM FROM ABUSE

As you step out from abuse, you will need support from other people. To start with, that may mean a professional counselor and one trusted friend or relative. Expect that these keys will work best when you involve other people.

1.   Admit that it happened and do not blame yourself.

2.   Be prepared to face the fact that the abuse has hurt you in some way – body, soul and spirit. And your identity has been damaged.

3.   Work through past pain with a professional counselor.

4.   Recognize how you self yourself, others and relationships.

5.   Explore the habits, attitudes and thought patterns you have developed, and be willing to change them if necessary.

6.   Discover the defense mechanisms you have adopted to stop yourself from being hurt, and adopt positive behaviors to help you deal with any future hurt.

7.   Learn to re-establish appropriate boundaries [see Chapter 11], with the help of others.

8.   Learn to forgive. This is for YOUR benefit and not just for the benefit of the person you are forgiving.

9.   Dare to begin to trust and love again, and allow yourself to be loved.

10. Reach out and help someone else. Use your past to give someone else hope for the future.

dignity

"One's dignity may be assaulted, vandalized and cruelly mocked, but it can never be taken away unless it is surrendered."[1]

Michael J. Fox

chapter fourteen

the mistress

secrets

secrets

secrets

When we think of a mistress or the 'other woman' we automatically think about a selfish woman of no moral fiber who is hell-bent on destroying a marriage and family. That might be the case, but what about the man involved? And what about this woman, the mistress? Who is she and what would cause her to live such a compromised life?

In her weekly Bible study blog, Liz Curtis Higgs shares the story of the Sinful Woman of Luke 7, drawn from the pages of her book, *Bad Girls of the Bible*, "We don't know her name, her age, or her history. We know only that she was bad for a season. To be specific, she sold her body for money. Because her sinful lifestyle was common knowledge, people whispered about her, eyed her with disdain, avoided her company.

Except Jesus.

He welcomed her touch.

He met her gaze.

He called her forgiven.

Here's the story: Simon, a Pharisee, invited Jesus to a large public dinner. In the style of the day, the Lord reclined at a low table, propping himself up on his left elbow, eating with his right hand. His body was stretched out, his feet exposed. Aha.

Then "a woman who had lived a sinful life in that town" (Luke 7:37) showed up at Simon's house. Make no mistake, she was "an especially wicked sinner" (AMP), "an immoral woman" (NLT). Her sins weren't listed in detail because they didn't need to be. The world's oldest profession hardly requires a job description.

She came alone, bearing a small alabaster vial of perfume. Did she intend to give the Lord this "flask of ointment" (AMP), this "jar of fragrant oil" (HCSB)? Or did she mean simply to anoint his head, a common gesture of respect?

Whatever her plans, they flew out the window the moment she saw him. Jesus.

Speechless, she drew closer, then "stood behind him at his feet weeping" (Luke 7:38). Little wonder. Tears often spring to my eyes when I sense the Lord's presence. Tears of sorrow for my sins. Tears of gratitude for his goodness.

Perhaps she felt the same.

Perhaps you've been there as well.

She cried so hard that "her tears began to wet his feet "(Luke 7:38 CJB). You know she must have been mortified. But she couldn't stop her tears—not when her heart was filled to overflowing. She sank to her knees, then bowed her head so low it touched the ground.

Jesus didn't pull away, didn't scold her, didn't make her feel foolish. No, he gladly received the baptism of her tears, recognizing this heartfelt expression for what it was- worship, pure and holy. She could have used her sleeves to dry his tear-drenched feet. Instead, "she wiped them with the hair of her head" (NKJV). Far more personal, more humble, more sacrificial.

Our Bad Girl held nothing back now. She pressed her lips to his feet, "kissing them many times" (NCV). Not just once in shy affection, but "over and over again" (GW) with an abundance born of passion. It was customary to kiss a man's hand or cheek or the hem of his garment. But this woman kissed his dirt-covered, stone-bruised feet.

Oh my.

And she wasn't finished yet.

Then she reached for her alabaster box, "and poured perfume" (Luke 7:38) on his feet—the same perfume she wore to advertise her services. So much for slipping under the radar at Simon's gathering.

When Mary of Bethany anointed Jesus on a later occasion, "the house was filled with the fragrance of the perfume" (John 12:3). This anointing, though, was done in a different time and place, and performed by a very different woman. Not Mary of Bethany, and certainly not Mary Magdalene, who has yet to be introduced in Luke's gospel and who was never called a prostitute anywhere in Scripture.

But this woman?

Undeniably bad.

Simon the Pharisee had seen enough. He said to himself, "If this man were a prophet, he would know who is touching him and what kind of woman she is—that she is a sinner" (Luke 7:39). He was not only disgusted with this "social outcast, devoted to sin" (AMP), he was also unimpressed with Jesus.

If he were a prophet...

Clearly Simon was not convinced.

Jesus knew the man's thoughts, and so responded with a story about two men in debt to a moneylender. One owed a lot, one owed a little. Neither man could afford to pay back his loan, so the moneylender canceled their debts and "freely forgave them both" (Luke 7:42 AMP).

Don't you love the Lord's teaching style? Enter into their story, he beckons. Learn from their example.

When Jesus asked Simon, "Which of them will love him more?" (Luke 7:42), the Pharisee had no choice but to confess, "I suppose the one he forgave more" (Luke 7:43 HCSB). Too right, Simon.

The Lord affirmed the man's answer, then turned toward our repentant Bad Girl, even as he continued speaking to Simon. This is my favorite part.

"Do you see this woman?" (Luke 7:44)

Simon saw a prostitute, period. He didn't see her as a person, nor had he "noticed" (CEV) her acts of worship for what they were.

But Jesus missed nothing. He saw her. He saw her sordid past, her humble present, and her glorious future. He quickly described all the ways she'd honored him—unlike Simon—then finished with this startling announcement: "Her sins, which are many, are forgiven" (Luke 7:47 ASV).

All her sins? All are forgiven? Yes. Why? "Because she loves much" (Luke 7:47 NLV)."[1]

Monique's Story ...

I remember...

At a very young age being made well aware that my masculine appearance had become a frequent source of negative attention.

I remember...

Feeling unfeminine, and believing that if I had just been born a male, all would be well within me.

I remember...

My humiliation as I was mistaken for a boy while in the Ladies Room, as I shamefully followed a grown woman's directions to a designated Men's Room.

I remember...

The stinging commentary as my sister describes her horror, when her friends mistook me for her little brother.

I remember...

The slow progression of my own bullying behavior, in an effort to crush the impending pain that was perpetually lurking, as my awkward appearance drew ridicule.

I remember...

Feeling misunderstood, like I didn't belong, like I was never enough, like I was always a disappointment.

Never enough, never enough - not pretty enough, not smart enough, not skinny enough, not rich enough – in anything – or in any way.

I remember...

The fleeting moments that crept in as my soul would scream, "I AM SPECIAL!" - yet not being able to find validation - anywhere.

I remember...

Saying my ritualistic bedtime prayers - as my sweet mother had instructed - not believing for a moment that God would hear my insignificant little voice.

I remember…

At age 13, taking my first hard alcoholic drink, in a desperate attempt to move out of my perpetual discomfort, not realizing that its darkness would only lead me further away from the path of my deepest desires.

Time marches on, and only my appearance begins to change – according to society, for the better. Amazingly, the very things about my young physique that brought me such pain, seemed to morph into the textbook look of a sinewy siren. My wide set shoulders became the frame for my once overly lanky limbs. My once too tall frame, (taller than every boy) was anchored by strong, athletic, attention drawing legs. My pronounced lips (for which I was teased relentlessly) somehow began to fit my maturing facial features. And, my once very, very thin physique began to blossom into a very noticeable likeness to my incredibly stunning mother. From age 14 to almost 16, I was sought after and accepted the attention of pretty much the entire football, basketball, and soccer teams. I engaged in ritual binge drinking and the sampling of illicit drugs - the darkness ever lurking - still no relief.

I remember…

Realizing that my sexuality could be used to manipulate boys, guys and then men. I could draw them in while keeping them at a safe distance, and always wanting more. A very dangerous game. Trading up as I saw it - I was never satisfied, even when they played by my rules.

I remember…

The moment I realized that I could catch the attention of an older man. Much too young to be aware of, and too innocent to conceive of - the irreparable damage and repercussions this path would hold.

Searching day and night for validation outside of myself - perhaps my heaven would be found in the love of a good man?

And so, the parade of men, and other women's men began. Nothing and no one was off limits - and I had perfected the art of appearing the "Innocent". Girlfriends and then wives would tell you otherwise. A tragic and shameful existence only deepened my sense of worthlessness.

I remember...

Partnering with wonderful young men in my early relationships. Fine, God fearing men, yet always older and more mature than my tender years. My restless fractured soul could not sustain a healthy relationship. My alcohol use was ever present, in an effort to stamp out the calling from the secret self-loathing that I carried within me - always. Why aren't they the answer? Why didn't being with them make me feel whole?

Despite every effort, they could never love me the right way, deeply enough, or strong enough for me to feel it - no matter how hard they tried, and oh how they tried. Sadly, these relationships were ended by me and only because of my inability to commit to a healthy, whole partnership. How could I, when I was secretly falling to pieces?

Perhaps more alcohol will help ease the emptiness? A terrible choice, as its use only deepens my sense of darkness. With my desire to get outside of myself intensifying, and substance use alone not taking me far enough, a devastating eating disorder soon finds a comfortable spot right next to my alcohol abuse, and now, I am even more empty - obsessed with improving my outward appearance. Perhaps then, when my body is perfect, I will attract the right man that will complete me and bring me peace?

So I move on - leaving broken hearts, still searching for that feeling - the one that is written about, the one that fairy tales are made of.

I remember...

After countless false starts along the way, at 24, entering into another relationship. He is 20 years my senior - I am easily lured in by the free flowing Champagne, Leer jets, endless drugs and a "Money Is No Object" lifestyle. Finally - someone to take care of me. Not so fast! At his direction, I take a devastating fall into six straight years of a new, and very severe drug habit, which I gladly accept, just to ease the perpetual discomfort in which I exist. Without the commitment of a marriage, I blindly move in with my provider - I am soon buried in unthinkable sexual demands and exposed to a perverse lifestyle that most times I could not even face. My drug use escalates. A stoned partner is a willing partner. Out of touch with reality, and digging a hole to darkness in which I am sure I will never return - exploited for my outward appearance, while silencing the cries of my heart with any and all drugs - a nasty and very expensive cocaine habit leaves me neatly tied to this man whom had no problem opening wide this door that I so willingly ran through. I would die in this situation if I didn't break away, as not using, is not an option in this household. But he was so good to me - he never hit me, he provided for me: he took care of me - he loves me – right? How could I live without him? And then, one night - another near overdose raised the stakes on my life, and I became a liability. Even he began to grow tired of my inability to keep within "reasonable ranges". Soon after a brush with an overdose, I make the decision to flee. He was not amused - he had heard this threat before. He soon crossed a dangerous line in a desperate attempt to keep me. I ran with nothing but the clothes on my back, as my poor parents received the call they'd been waiting for, and dreaded at the same time – that I was coming home. I was 29.

I pray to this God that I hear about, to take me - as I felt I was not worth saving. Extremely risky behavior became my mantra as I begged God to take me away from my misery - and still I lived - but why?

The God I knew is full of judgment, and expectations - and how could He love ME anyway, when I was so lost and broken?

A pitiful time followed as I confessed my regrets and owned up to my addictions. I decide that the love for my parents and the pain I have caused would be enough to help me get and stay clean - I was very mistaken. Prescription drugs and alcohol nicely took the place of my illegal cocaine use but did equal damage when used together. Therapists deemed me a difficult case. I was labeled with a plethora of psychology terms, and relied on a particular therapist who had clearly developed his own fascination with my book-worthy life. Therapy consisted of two to three weekly sessions, and ever increasing doses of medications, but never a dose of spirituality.

Within a few short weeks, I was arrested for DUI, and left in a very unpleasant jail cell by the man that had claimed to love me for six years. That was the final chapter in that relationship, and my chronic use of cocaine. I had put my poor parents through enough.

My beautiful parents, God loving and fearing people. Equipped only with great love for their child, and the limited tools that religion had given them - they watched in horror as I continued to self-destruct.

I remember...

Men, men everywhere.

Everywhere there were men, and I felt the need to be adored by each and every one of them. Older, younger, available, especially if they were not - wouldn't the risk the unavailable would have to take to be with me, mean they REALLY love me? I welcomed all men and searched for validation in the arms of too many to count.

I remember...

The appearance of a promising relationship - at last - my wish had been granted. He was 21 years my senior. A kind wonderful man who took amazing care of my heart, and my life. With sheer determination, I kicked the drugs, but the alcohol was an integral part of our relationship.

He too had a secret to hide. He belonged to another woman. Our bond was very deep, very quickly. The highs were like nothing I'd ever experienced, and the thought of my life without him seemed unimaginable. I awaited word of his impending divorce only to be met with the news that his wife was ill, very ill – dying of cancer – and that our life together as promised, would need to be postponed until she was well enough to take "the change". So I waited - all the while falling more deeply in love as I watched him try to "do the right thing". Her very survival was tenuous, and his dedication to her care, while caring for me, only pulled me deeper into this impossible situation. We decided to keep our relationship a secret in an effort to minimize her pain - my pain however grew exponentially as I perfected the art of cheating by watching him – the master. Each time he went back to her I attempted to kill the pain by using another. Countless men crossed my doorstep, but they were never enough. Never enough. The pain of my shame only deepened. Promises made and promises broken rolled into eight long years of waiting and hoping, still looking for him to finally make me happy. His financial commitment was unparalleled, and very hard to escape. Our passion and drive to experience this life together unveiled glorious adventures that invariably ended with his return to her, and a pain of loss that cannot be described. The price became too high, the despair is too much - with nowhere to turn, I relieved the pain by secretly cutting myself, ritually drinking to blackouts, chain smoking of cigarettes, and a daily pleading with God to please just let it be over.

And then, in a final failed attempt to actively end my life, a botched hanging attempt leaves me desperately wondering, why God wouldn't even take me?

An ALL time low ensued.

In a moment of clarity, I foresaw the ending of yet another "forever" relationship. My heart was broken, looking for anything to fill this void that had wholly swallowed me, heart and soul. At this point, you would think that one would recognize this ongoing pattern of relational destruction? But not me. Instead, the most complicated relationship of my life was about to be born.

I remember...

With my alcohol abuse in full swing and my eating and image issues consuming my every waking moment, a fascinating yet wounded and volatile man walked straight into my life. He is flanked by beautiful little souls – his very young children. Finally, I recognized someone that was in more pain than me; a man, a family that I can save and call my own. I believed that loving him enough would help us both. We could get well together. Soon I realized that the blind cannot lead the blind - and his sickness was profoundly more damaging than the state in which I had learned to exist. I almost immediately become his soldier, immersing myself in all aspects of his life. If I did well, I figured that there must be a happy ending here - right? His very difficult life became our main focus, and my usefulness became painfully apparent. I was stripped of my dignity; my self-esteem so low, that I was easily manipulated into bringing in money to support our family by any and all means. Past relationships, new acquaintances, selling off my things, and essentially, prostituting myself.

I was bullied into turning over my life savings, as guilt was a common weapon. When that didn't work, escalating violent interactions became a familiar theme. I fought back, with my own brand of violence, but could never outwit, out speak, out fight, or out run him - spitting in my face, and berating me were never off limits. We were very careful to shield the children from what had become our norm, and in their presence, we played happy family, as best we could. Years of even harder drinking and mounting debt brought us to an all time low that should have been the beginning of the end, but instead the true violence now begins. My combative behavior fueled an already dangerous situation. I was anything but a victim. I was a willing participant in our perpetual battles.

New designer drugs were used as a way to unveil my secrets, giving him greater power over me. Emotional blackmail, destroying of property, and open threats become a reality. One evening while passed out, I was pulled out of bed by my hair and dragged into a locked bathroom where the verbal assault began, and crescendos with a new level of violence. On my knees, as I caught my breath, I begged him to let me go, but he was not yet finished. The horror continued. I tried to fight back, but to no avail. As the authorities arrived, I contritely apologized for their trouble, and once again felt ashamed of my part in this humiliating situation. I was at his mercy, as I learned to take it with the help of more substance.

I remember…

Prescription meds - mood changers, spirit killers, I was dangerously close to going down, never to get up again. I knew I must leave, but first I must be able to think clearly. How could I leave my home – these beautiful children. How could I not? I know I must quit all substance – perhaps this would help our failing relationship? If I could only be a better person, then he would really love me. So the agonizing decision for sobriety was born.

One Christmas Eve I decide it was time. For the following six months, I'm quite sure I experienced hell on earth. All of the things I had heard were true – it is unbelievably painful physically, but the emotional pain is indescribable, with no possible coping mechanism. This new season brought us strangely closer together – both of us sober, both of us trying to better our lives – or so I thought. His commitment to a better life looked very different than mine. About a year later, I was certain that I would need something other than a man to strengthen my belief in myself. Could it be – God – after all?

Not if he could help it.

After all, Jesus was off limits – and a very dangerous area in which to tread. I had been warned.

I remember…

The difficulties of maintaining sobriety for three long years, with nothing by my own strong will. The children became my main motivation, but I was still certain that there must be a deeper purpose, and meaning surrounding my journey.

I will never forget…

My first connection with a true woman of God – my suspicion and fear in a heightened state. I had been warned repeatedly about THESE people, yet with goose bumps still raised I saw the light of the Holy Spirit in her eyes, and felt the presence of God in my soul. I simply had to find out more about this inexplicable pull towards the light. Could this be the God that I had never known? I would have to meet with her in secret – the danger factor was increasing at just the mention of the name of Jesus Christ.

Gently she sat with me, on my terms, in her time, sharing stories of the Gospel. Riveted, I sat in her presence and was awestruck by what seemed to be her genuine love of Jesus first and then, a wretch like me. Months of watching from a safe distance turned into an acceptance of Jesus in my heart, a day that began my transformation from total darkness into indescribable light. My dearest friend never told me, but rather showed me the love of Jesus – through her actions. My faith grew stronger, and stronger, as did I. And now armed with truth, and an unshakable relationship with God, I have been blessed with a new outlook, and a new happy – God filled life.

No drugs, no alcohol, no medications, no therapists – only Jesus.

Grounded in God, I will not be moved.

I have peace.

Peace.

You too can write your own ending.

Mine looks something like this.

JESUS LOVES.

JESUS SAVES.

HAPPILY EVER AFTER.

TO BE CONTINUED.

THE END.

5 KEYS TO MOVING ON AFTER AN AFFAIR

1.   **If Your Husband Has An Affair.**

The first thing to do is forgive him. That will set your heart free to make wise decisions. Take your time in making any decision that will affect your future. His choice in being unfaithful is enough without you adding any further unwise choices. Don't seek revenge. Don't stalk social media. Exercise discipline in guarding your heart and your mind. Pray and ask God to help guide you. Seek help from family and friends you can trust. Don't be alone. Cry and process but don't wallow in self-pity. There is hope, so hold on tight to it.

2.   **If You Have An Affair as a Married Woman.**

The first thing to do is stop! Then seek forgiveness from God, and from the person you have been unfaithful with. Cut all ties, physical and emotional, with them immediately. Don't think back, look back, hope back, go back. You also need to confess to your spouse and seek their forgiveness. Allow them time to process, just as you would appreciate the time to process. Forgiving yourself is probably going to be the hardest thing to do, but it is essential if you are going to move on and rebuild your future.

3.   **How to Affair Proof Your Life.**

Stay very closely connected to your spouse. Keep the intimate aspects of your relationship private between the two of you. If you share intimate details of your relationship with other people, they are no longer intimate. Talk with your spouse. Keeping an uncluttered line of communication between the two of you is essential. Plan date nights, date lunches, play days and make sure you don't crowd them out of your calendar. Your kids are important but not more important than your marriage. Spend time with everyone you love and you will find a great balance that will bring health to your spouse and kids. Finally, and importantly, enjoy sex and lots of it!

4.   **How to Help Kids Affected by Infidelity.**

Minimize drama. Maximize hope. Infidelity is not the end of a marriage and family. The end of a marriage is, usually, because of irreconcilable differences. When both partners are willing to forgive and move on, there is hope. As I learned with my first marriage, I couldn't make my spouse's decisions for him and sadly our marriage ended. That, however, didn't give me a license to use my personal pain and grief to turn my children's lives upside down, or to try to turn them against their father. Weathering the storm of infidelity can result in a safe landing or it can shipwreck little lives. Choose love. For the sake of your children, please choose love. It never fails.

5.   **How to Help a Friend or Family Member.**
By all means, please be a support, especially if you have been invited to do so. If, however, you are observing a friend or family member weather through infidelity, it is important not to interfere. Intervention is a tough call and should be reserved for those you are in very close relationship with, otherwise your intervention strategy will be deemed as interference. Go carefully and PRAY!!

chapter fifteen

worth the wait

wait

wait

wait

When I married Jonathan William Wilson on April 5th, 1997, I inherited a beautiful young woman – his daughter – Rachel Claire Wilson. She was twelve years old at the time, sixteen years my junior. I always wanted to have four kids, and I knew that Rachel was a daughter I had prayed for.

I loved her then.

I love her now.

She was a tweenager when she first came into my life and I can now say that I have successfully raised a teenage daughter. Phew. Applause later, please. Much of my success as Rachel's Mum is due to Rachel. I wasn't handed a handbook when I was handed this child. I had no clue what to do except that I had prayed for four children, and she was one of them. So I figured I would be her Mum, plain and simple. That meant not trying to win her approval or to become her best friend. I had to become her Mum. Rachel had a Mum, so I knew I wasn't meant to be her, but she needed another Mum, and I knew I could be her. Parenting requires space invading. I know not to abdicate my role as a parent, for to do so is to leave a child without measure. As a parent, abdication is never an option. We need to adjust and redirect, not just correct.

At the age of fourteen Rachel came home one night after Youth at church to announce that she had a boyfriend, to which I responded, "No you don't." to which Rachel responded, "Ok." Wow, could parenting really be this simple? I wish! Rachel just happened to be a dream daughter who genuinely wanted to do the right thing. She was a normal teenage girl in every sense but without the need for exploring reckless rebellion. I will forever be grateful for the gift this young woman has been in my life.

When Rachel turned twenty-one, I can recall thinking that I needed to start reversing some of my prayers. I had asked God to protect her and keep her, and He had. She was (and still is) stunningly beautiful inside and out, and she had plenty of attention coming her way. Rachel had learned to say no and learned to make choices that would cause her to have less crowd friends and more dear friends. One evening she arrived home from work and sat on the end of my bed as she had become accustomed to doing over the years. She had shared so vulnerably that she was feeling lonely. She had made choices about friends that would cause her to be left of out of some fun circles. She had made choices not to date around. Now she was wondering what would become of her future. I assured her that God had a magnificent plan for her life that would only involve His best. She went to bed, and I went to God. "Father please let him come soon. Let him sweep her off her feet because you have swept him off his. Nothing less please Lord. I love you. Amen."

We were in the midst of a massive life transition for our family as we were about to move from Sydney, Australia to Newport Beach, California to start a brand new church – Newport Church. The announcement was made on Thanksgiving 2005, and we needed to start building our new church family. We started to host parties at our home in Sydney so that we could share the vision, and feed our new family. Our new team consisted of young American Bible College Students who were returning to the United States to start something new. We shared the vision, and they jumped on board. One young man who was part of our original start up crew was Jamin Steel, a fine looking young man with a heart of gold, and gifted to change this world. I knew he and Rachel liked each other and prayed that somehow that they could fall in love and live happily ever after. Jamin visited our home many times, mostly to help us build our team, and also to court our daughter. I remember cooking breakfast for Jamin one morning that he was visiting before taking Rachel out ice-skating. I said, "Jamin, no boy, guy or man apart from her father has ever held Rachel's hand. And Jamin, no one has ever broken her heart. No pressure, but please do not hurt her!" He knew the seriousness of his pursuit of her and we deeply appreciated his care and concern.

Rachel is a dreamer who loves to dream. She's a very beautiful person, but she was as tempted as anybody else to fall for anyone else, to chase anyone else, and to have it all done and sewed up, quickly and early, and she just didn't. She denied herself to the point of loneliness. She paid then, and she plays now. She is now living the dream because she chose to not sell out for Mr. Wrong because she wasn't prepared to wait for Mr. Right. Jamin asked Jonathan if he could befriend Rachel. The answer was yes. Jamin asked Jonathan if he could date Rachel. The answer was yes. Jamin finally asked Jonathan if he could marry Rachel. The answer was a loud and resounding yes and amen! On September 13th, 2007 they both said, "I do." Daughter number one was signed, sealed and delivered.

There is a vast difference between a boy, a guy, and a man. You don't want to marry a really nice boy. You give birth to a boy; you don't want to marry one. You don't want to marry a really nice guy. Is that guy the kind of person you see raising your children? You actually want a man – you need a man. Whether you have been married 50 years or you're still in high school, we need to understand that God wants us to wise up. God does not choose our mate for us. He might have certain people in his mind that would be like a perfect match, but ultimately we make the decision; we're the one that says I do. We choose our partner, and if you have been down the aisle once or twice, or it doesn't matter how many times, you understand the certain uncertainty of that walk. And you know enough to recognize unwise seasons of your life.

There is a certain uncertainty when walking down the aisle on your wedding day. No one really knows how everything is going to work out. There is much hope of course, but at the end of the day a marriage is joining two people together. And two people will always have two wills. And where there is a will, there will always be a way. However, where there is one willing and one not, there is very little the willing one can do. We must trust God. There are some too afraid to take that walk. They are afraid to walk that risk. They are afraid to lean. We shouldn't fall for a guy. We should lean towards a man of God. The initial lean can be daunting but remember that it is just a lean – so don't fall, yet. Whatever happens, don't fall in love until you have leaned in for a significant amount of time. That amount of time is different for everyone, but allow enough time to get to know each other in usual and unusual settings, with family and friends, old and new.

sex

"May your fountain, your sex life, be blessed by God; may you know true joy with the wife of your youth."

proverbs chapter five verse eighteen
[the voice]

let's talk about sex

by Kerri Weems

sex

sex

sex

The following chapter is an adaptation from a presentation made by Pastor Kerri Weems at IMAGINE Conference, October 2012.

I want you to know that I'm not a sex expert, and I won't be able to speak to every single one of your situations. I am just one woman who has had lots of practice with one man, my husband. We're going to cover this topic from both an eternal and temporal perspective before we dig into Five Myths about Sex and Marriage. My goal is to arm you with some God-thoughts about sexuality so that you won't be vulnerable to the schemes of the enemy in this area. If you're already strong here, hopefully, this will strengthen you more. If you got some gaps to fill, hopefully, this will fill some gaps. If you need a perspective shift, I'm hoping to shift some perspective for you.

I know our sexuality is as varied as the number of people reading this book. That's how it's supposed to be - completely unique for each of us. When we talk about sex and sexuality there can be a tendency for some of us to close down, because this may be an area that brings pain to your memory. It's, unfortunately, the way that the enemy has come against women for the totality of history. Please know that I'm not trying to speak to the pain of this area of your life. As you read this chapter, I ask you to try to step outside of that pain for a moment, and allow me speak to the potential of sex in your life. Not the pain, but the potential. God wants this area of your life to blessed as much as He wants any other area of your life to be blessed.

ETERNITY

You are a triune being. You have a body, a soul and a spirit. At all times, every day, you are all three of these things. You are a physical being; you are an emotional, mental, intellectual being, and you are a spiritual being. You're also a product of eternity, placed in time, and in that place of time you experience seasons in life. You live in time and season, and you will live in eternity.

When we experience sex, we experience it not just in our bodies, but also in our souls. The act of sex points to eternity. If we fail to consider this, and only focus on the biological or psychological aspects, we will be shortchanged in this area of our lives.

Let's step back and take a panoramic view at sex. We're going to step back and look at eternity first, to find out God's original intent for sex, and what that means to us now. And then we're going to step into time, because even though our sexuality points towards eternity, we experience it in time. And in case you were wondering, when we go to heaven we will not be having sex. There are some religions that believe that, but Christianity is not one of them. There was a time when I struggled with that a little. I thought, "That's unfortunate It's one of the best things of my life right now on earth, and I will be sad to give it up." The fact is that we aren't going to miss it at all because sex is an earthly shadow of something real in eternity. It answers a time bound and earthly need that is not going to be a need in eternity. Just as in the Old Testament the sacrifices of that time pointed toward the future sacrifice of Jesus Christ, it was an earthly shadow of a heavenly reality. There is something that sex does for our soul and spirit here on earth that will be fulfilled completely in the presence of God in our eternal home.

BRIDEGROOM & BRIDE

God could have chosen to represent Christ's relationship to us in lots of different ways, and He does, but one of the primary ways that he represents Jesus to us, is as a bridegroom coming back for his bride.

In the gospel of John, in the account of the Last Supper, we see that Jesus comforted His disciples with some words that were very common for a bridegroom to say to his bride. He tells them "In my

Father's house are many rooms. And I'm going away to prepare a place for you so that where I am you may be also." When a young bridegroom became to a woman and was about to then go back to his family's village, he would say the very same thing. By using those words Jesus was pointing toward Eternity, and He was building up a metaphor of husband and wife, or bridegroom and bride. The Apostle Paul says that marriage represents the relationship between Christ and the Church. Marriage is a sacrament. It's something that is holy.

GOD'S DESIGN FOR MARRIAGE

The first few chapters of Genesis give us many insights into the eternal, theological and spiritual nature of sexuality.

Moses wrote these chapters to answer two important questions:
1. Who is God?
2. Who is man in relation to God?

Genesis 1:27 says, "So God created mankind in his own image. In the image of God he created them." Here we see that God took himself, his own image, the image of one God, and he made two expressions of it. He made male and he made female. One God, two images. As the verse says, "God blessed them and said to them, 'Be fruitful and multiply.''

In Genesis chapter 2, we read that God caused Adam to fall into a deep sleep. Then, taking a rib out of Adam's side, God fashions Eve. God then brings Eve to Adam. We see Adam's response in verse 23, "...this is now bone of my bones and flesh of my flesh. She shall be called Woman for she was taken out of Man." This is a beautiful piece of poetry in the original Hebrew, with a beautiful rhythm to it that we miss in the English translation. When Adam sees Eve, he sees a part of himself and what he is really saying in verse 23 is, "Eve is an extension of my strength, bone of my bone; and flesh of my flesh, an extension of my heart." This is where we get the term "soul mate."

God's design for marriage is to bring these two aspects of His image back together so that His image can be complete again. It's pretty incredible that God did that. Why didn't he just make the one person to represent his image, which would have been a lot less complicated for us, right? But if you notice in the very beginning of this story, God said, "Let us make man in our image." God was not alone. He exists Father, Son, and Holy Spirit. Forever and always.

God is a relational God. And for man to fully reflect the nature of God, he had to be in relationship with someone compatible to him. When God brought the animals to Adam in Genesis 2:18-20, it became very clear to Adam that none of those were his equals, and he couldn't truly have a relationship with any of them. We are separate and distinct from other parts of creation, just as God is separate and distinct from humanity. We are not one and the same.

When God brought Woman to Adam, it was a different experience from his encounter with the animals. Adam saw that here in Eve was an extension of his strength, and an extension of his heart. When he saw her, he could see part of himself. God's intent was to bring his image back to full expression when man and woman became one flesh. His image was put back together in one sense, and it gave Him pleasure to do that because then man could know the joy of existing in relationship.

NAKED & UNASHAMED

In verse 25, we read that Adam and his wife were both naked, and they felt no shame. The Hebrew for shame also means embarrassment, disappointment and delay. Their nakedness was not a source of embarrassment. We need to understand that sexuality and God are not at odds with each other. It is sin that God is at odds with. God is not at odds with sex in the right context and in the right place. We have sowed this dichotomy between God and sex that God never intended. Sex is a very powerful spiritual reality in our lives. Adam and Eve were not ashamed or disappointed in what they saw. They were happy with what they saw, and they did not delay. In other words, if you were watching a movie today this would be where clothes start falling off, and people start rolling into bed. That's what the Bible tells us. They got busy, multiplying and filling the earth right then and there. It wasn't a shameful thing in any way, and they didn't see it as being at odds with God.

What has caused us to leave God out of our sexuality and bring him into all the other parts of our lives? The truth is that you are body, soul, and spirit. Your spirit doesn't go away when you are having sex. It remains. God doesn't close his eyes and look the other way when you are in the bedroom. He is looking at you. He is not ashamed of it. I'm sorry if that freaks you out. It shouldn't! You don't become unspiritual because you are in bed. Sex is a spiritual act, and it was always meant to be a spiritual act.

TIME

Now let's move from Eternity into Time, because that's where we live. We live in time and season. I have observed that people can sometimes go to extremes when it comes to dealing with their sexuality. Unable to process all that they are feeling, they may respond by erring either on the side of extreme repression or extreme expression.

Repression, acting like you can somehow take your sexuality out of you and put it in the freezer, pretending it is not there, is totally unrealistic. On the other hand, we also don't want to fall into an extreme of expression. Extreme expression does whatever it needs to in order to find some kind of relief or pleasure. None of us want to be on either one of those extremes. We want to be somewhere in the middle. In the middle is where life is.

There are some things that people commonly, but mistakenly believe about sex and marriage that aren't helpful to them or their spouse [or future spouse!]. Whether you're single or have been married now for some time, this next section is filled with very practical truths and is sure to help dispel some of those common myths about sex and marriage.

FIVE MYTHS ABOUT SEX AND MARRIAGE

1.   **My sex life pre-marriage won't affect my sex life post-marriage.**

We know what God intended sex to be, a rejoining of His two images together to create a whole. When you have sex with someone, and ideally it's supposed to be the first time you have sex with your spouse, your body creates a hormone rush, and you imprint on that person. Psychologists describe it as "sex glue." It's supposed to glue you to your mate emotionally and psychologically. It is supposed to hold you and bind you to the person you experience sex with. However, the more that we glue ourselves to different people, the more we lose our stickiness. The glue loses its ability to hold.

If you've ever used adhesive tape, you will know that it loses its stickiness the more surfaces you apply it to and rip it off from. In a similar way, the more people that we have sex with, the more we diminish our ability to bond.

The belief that we need to experience multiple partners to find out if we're compatible is a complete myth that the enemy has fed to us to make sure that we don't stay with anyone. The enemy wants to ensure that our chances of bonding with one person are diminished greatly. The myth is perpetuated by a fear and a worry that we're missing out on better sex with someone else.

For those of you who are single, I want you to know that I

empathize with you. I don't think that our bodies were meant to be single and celibate for 30 years. We experience puberty at around the age of 12, and 18 years of celibacy is not ideal. My personal opinion, not because I'm Southern but because I understand biology and how our body works, is that it's good to get married early. It's unfortunate that our culture has extended adolescence out so long that now people have to wait until they're 30 years old to have sex if they want to do things God's way.

To all the single people reading this, I say: You need to get married. You do! I know a lot of women would say, "Girl - I would get married if I could find the right man, but there are no good men around here." Let's back up. Girls come up to me sometimes, and they tell me, "Oh, I just admire you and Pastor Stovall's marriage so much, you have the best marriage. I really want to marry a man just like Pastor Stovall. Please tell me how I can become the woman I need to be so I can marry someone like that." This is what I always say to them. "I'll let you in on a secret. He wasn't like this when I married him. He was 25 years old. Do you know what 25-year-old guys are like? They're not like 45-year-old guys. My husband is the man he is today because I married him. It's the truth. And I'm the woman I am today because I married him." What people see in my husband and me today is the result of a lifetime of us growing toward each other, not apart from each other.

My observation is that most single girls today want to marry a 45-year-old man in a 25-year-old body. But the reality is, when you marry a 25-year-old body, you get a 25-year-old man! It means that he may not be mature enough to focus fully on you when you interrupt his football game to talk about your feelings. He might not like to go shopping at the latest shoe boutique. Yes, there are some men that like to do that, but they're probably not the men you want to marry.

We have a disease among women of perfectionism. We expect perfection for ourselves, and we, in turn expect perfection in our man.

I'm not suggesting that we settle for the first man that pops the question. Let's not do that. Please don't settle - don't marry someone who's not saved, and please don't marry someone who has anger or control issues. However, DO remember that you are marrying potential, not perfection. Let's not be fear driven or perfectionistic when it comes to choosing who we will marry.

While we're talking about time and sexuality and real life, here's something to think about: there is a time in your life when it is easy to meet other single people, and then there's a time when it's not easy. When you're in that time, meet, marry, do it. Don't over think it. Get over yourself. So the guy burps. Big deal; you burp. So he toots; you toot. So he has hobbies; you have hobbies as well. Find some non-negotiables, but not 20 non-negotiables. Maybe three or four. Five at the most. A "God first" attitude and lifestyle needs to be your number one non-negotiable, not their job or economics. Make sure they are devoted to the House of God.

Then of course there are other filters that you can pick for yourself, but when you make your list of non-negotiables, please do not make your ideal version of your best girl friend with "male parts." Don't. There are men that fit that description. Again - you do not want to marry those men. We don't want to bring the same two components of God's image together. Let him be who he is. Let them be masculine, and you feminine.

And to the men who are reading this, you need to marry someone for their heart rather than their body, because everybody looks good when they're 25, but bodies change as we age. You could marry the hottest girl today, and then later on when she has babies she could look completely different.

Your sex life before you get married does impact your marriage. So please, let's set ourselves up for a win. Let's stop trying to be such perfectionists that we screen out and dismiss every guy.

2.   Married sex is a cure for lust.

This is false. Married sex is not, and will never be a cure for lust because lust is a spiritual issue. Many people think that they'll quit struggling with lust if they can just get married, but the truth is that lust follows us into our marriages if we don't have a proper handle on it. Lust can destroy a marriage because it is something that focuses on selfish gain. It doesn't look to meet the needs of the spouse.

Our minds are incredibly malleable, and sexual arousal is one of the most powerful ways that we can imprint on our brains. Most of us realize that there are certain images we shouldn't look at, but there are also books that we would be wise to steer clear of, no matter how popular they are in our culture. Just because there aren't any pictures in the book doesn't mean it is not porn. Looking outside of our spouse for arousal creates a bond with the source of the arousal. That weakens our ability to bond with our spouse.

You might be married and may feel like your sex life is fizzling a bit. Everyone around you might be turning to certain things to add some spice, but you don't need to get on that train. Once you get on that train, you probably won't be able to get off of it without some help. Just remind yourself, nothing's worth the weakening of your bond with your spouse. Nothing's worth it.

3.   Married sex is boring.

That is not true!

I was talking with a great single friend of mine about this. She's in her early 30's and let me know that she and her single friends often wonder what married sex must be like after many years of marriage. They wonder how do you 'keep sex hot' for 18 years? That question shows such a wrong idea of it, actually. The goal of sex isn't hotness. The goal of sex is not excitement. The goal of sex is love.

If the goal of your sex life is for it to be greater, and crazier, and wilder and hotter every time, you're going to be disappointed. What are you going to end up doing? Swing from the chandelier in your bedroom? How far are you going to take it? There are limits, and we must have a bigger goal than excitement.

The bigger goal is love. Sex is about love. The goal of married sex is cementing your marriage. The goal is to bring strength and add unity. The goal is to bring the image of God back together. Sex is very spiritual.

It's important to remember that sex is about more than our physical body. While you're in your teen years and your early 20's, your hormones are raging, and all you can think about is your body. The fact is that your body will get old. It won't work the same at 45 as it did at 25. Then it won't work the same at 65 as it did at 45. It is a body planted in time that eventually will not be useful for those things. Thankfully, sex is not only about your body; it's also about your soul and your spirit. If we nurture the psychological and spiritual aspects of sex, we can carry those things with us as we age.

As wives, we should be careful to guard this area of our lives. We must not hold it lightly. I'm not saying that you need to have sex with your husband every single night. You're free to say no. I don't want to make anyone feel guilty if you're not having sex a certain number of times per week. There's no pressure. Neither spouse should just do whatever they want, whenever they want to, at the expense of the other person. On the other hand, we need to be careful about constantly shutting down this aspect of our marriage because of fatigue or because we're unhappy with our bodies.

Body image can be a real issue when it comes to sex, especially after we have kids, and our bodies have changed so much. Many of us even feel self-conscious about our bodies before we have kids. When we don't take care of that aspect of ourselves, and we face challenges regarding body image, our tendency can be to shut down sexually in marriage. Consider this: there's probably no other time in your marriage, no other place, that your husband feels as loved and honored and respected as he does in the bedroom.

I'm not saying that to put pressure on anyone, or to over-spiritualize sex. I'm simply saying that it's very important to him. It is too important, in fact, for you to make a habit of saying no to him because you're tired. Or for you not to take care of health issues, or deal with any psychological hang ups or constructs that you've built throughout the years about sex that are hindering you in this area. You need to seek the help you need to seek. Sex is too important, and it has the capacity to make or break your marriage.

I always say, "Sex is not a big deal until it's a big deal." When it's in its proper place and its proper time, it shouldn't be a big deal. But when it starts to get out of whack, it becomes a big deal. It really does. So we need to guard the area of our hearts where our sexuality resides.

4.   Sex and love are not the same things.

Outside of marriage, that is true. They're not the same thing. Within marriage, however, they should be. God gave us this thing called sex for the temporal period of time in which we live on earth. We're not going to have it in eternity. Even within the parentheses of time, God took it yet further, and he limited it to one specific context - the context of marriage. That is the only place that we find his blessing raining down over it because it points to eternity.

The most important prayer that the Israelites prayed was, "Hear O Israel, the Lord your God is one God." Deuteronomy 6:4. God wanted Israel to know, "I'm one God. And I'm the only God that you should serve, there's no other besides Me, and I'm completely devoted to you. In spite of your flaws and in spite of the ways that you betray Me time and time again there is a safety in the commitment of covenant." Covenant is the place where our most vulnerable moments are meant to be expressed. When they are expressed outside of that covenant of commitment, it hurts us and fractures the image of God. Now, can God rebuild? 100% yes, but let's be intentional about not using for another purpose what God intended for covenant.

I was not 100% perfect in this area prior to meeting and marrying my husband. He certainly wasn't perfect either. Very few people are. That's why we all need to rely on the grace and redemptive power of Jesus! When God saves us He reconstructs His image and makes it beautiful and un-fragmented in Christ. None of us, from the least of us to the greatest, from the most moral and upright to the worst sinner – none of us could bridge the gap of Heaven without the Cross. All of us are fragmented and need to be reconstructed. God is too good! He redeems and can totally put all of our broken pieces back together in wholeness.

That's what grace is.

5.   Sex is for procreation, not pleasure.

Not true.

The end.

CONCLUSION: A HIGHER PURPOSE

Let's step back into Eternity again. In 1 Corinthians 6, we read a letter that the Apostle Paul has written to the church in Corinth to deal with the issue of sexual immorality. That isn't just a modern problem that we face; it was a problem back then too.

The people in Corinth had reduced their sexuality to a bodily function, just like using the toilet or eating or drinking. If we believe that sex is merely something we have to do because we're human, then we focus solely on the biology of it. The Corinthians had taken the psychology and the spirituality out of it.

Many of us are like the Corinthians. We may think, "Stay out of my sex life – it's my right, it's my body and I can do whatever I want with it." Paul's message to them is, "No, I'm not staying out of your sex life. It's my place as your pastor and your leader to help you reconstruct the image that God imprinted on you."

Paul says that our bodies were not made for sexual immorality. He says that our bodies were made for the Lord. Your body has a purpose beyond sex. You may have a big sex drive – that's normal, and biological – but let me tell you what your body was really made for. You're made with purpose, and this is the purpose that you're made for: to be a temple of the Holy Spirit. Your body was made to house the presence of God. And temples are holy. Not because of the construct, but because of the God that inhabits it.

Your body was made so that you could carry the presence of God to your world. Stewarding your sexuality is ultimately about honoring the temple where God lives, and understanding that we don't segment ourselves into the categories of body, soul, and spirit. Our spirit and the Holy Spirit live inside a temple. It matters what we do with our body because our bodies are holy. We're carrying the presence of God with us everywhere we go.

That is important for us to remember beyond the subject of sex – it's applicable to all areas of our life. Managing your sexuality is not about having a list of rules to follow. It's about understanding that you carry the presence of God with you. Whatever season you find yourself in, steward your body in order to carry the presence of God well.

choices

"You say, "I am allowed to do anything"—but not everything is good for you. And even though "I am allowed to do anything," I must not become a slave to anything. You say, "Food was made for the stomach, and the stomach for food." (This is true, though someday God will do away with both of them.) But you can't say that our bodies were made for sexual immorality. They were made for the Lord, and the Lord cares about our bodies."

one corinthians chapter six verses twelve to thirteen
[new living translation]

anger management

By Robert M. Fraum, Ph.D

Does your partner have excessive anger or problems coping with their anger? Does their manner of expressing anger cause harm to you or those you care about? Are there signs that you need help dealing with your anger? Dr. Robert M. Fraum, Ph.D., a licensed New York psychologist who provides anger management therapy explains the differences between normal anger and anger management problems.

HEALTHY ANGER

Healthy anger is deliberate, proportional, and responsive to a clear and present need. Healthy anger is a powerful tool of human survival and adaptation. It is functional and in the service of valid goals. Anger becomes dysfunctional when it works against our best interests or our higher values.

THE FEELING OF ANGER

The feeling of anger is an emotional component of an instinctive physiological reaction. It is also an inner signal that something may be wrong. Our intuition may be informing us to watch out, or to assert ourselves, or to protect others. For example, we may get angry or express anger if we see someone harming a defenseless child.

REACTIVE OR IMPULSIVE ANGER

Reactive or impulsive anger may help us at these times to do the right thing automatically. Usually it doesn't. It just hurts others and gets us in trouble.

CHANNELIZED OR SUBLIMINATED ANGER

Channelized or sublimated anger is a type of healthy anger. It is anger that has been redirected from its original source into socially acceptable forms of expression, like aggressive sports, political blogging, or chopping wood.

DEFINITION OF AN ANGER CONTROL PROBLEM

Anger control problems, anger disorders, and anger management problems refer to dysfunctional patterns in the way we handle or use anger. "Dysfunctional anger" does not help us to do the right thing. Dysfunctional anger can be destructive, out of proportion, and inappropriate to the circumstances. Often, it is unnecessary and harmful to others. An anger management problem also arises when we get angry too often, even if we only upset ourselves. Angry feelings and aggressive behavior do not necessarily indicate a problem with anger. However, there is a problem if anger is too intense or powerful, lasts to long, or occurs to often, or inappropriate to the circumstances. When a pattern of anger or aggressive behavior interferes with our lives or harms others, we are dealing with an anger disorder or an anger management problem.

TYPES OF ANGER MANAGEMENT PROBLEMS

There are many patterns and types of anger problems but no comprehensive psychiatric typology for anger. So I will approach the issue of types of anger from several psychological perspectives. We can describe types of anger in behavioral, emotional, or interpersonal terms. In addition, some anger control problems are symptoms of a psychological disorder. The following descriptions may give you a clearer sense of what kind of anger you are dealing with or observing.

UNHEALTHY STYLES OF EXPRESSING AND MANAGING ANGER

Here are some ways of dealing with harmful anger, especially as an ingrained habit, expressive style, or a defensive coping mechanism.

BEHAVIORAL AGGRESSION

Behavioral aggression describes anger that is expressed in physical behaviors towards people or destruction of property. Aggressive behaviors, like domestic violence, fist fights, aggressive driving, and road rage are relatively infrequent for most people. However, they can have frightening, harmful, or deadly consequences. They can also generate an automatic response from law enforcement or child or adult protective service professionals.

VERBAL ABUSE

Verbal abuse includes temper tantrums, verbal rage reactions, bullying, intimidation, and brow beating. These are much more common. They can result in divorce, in a civil law suit or an official, or in an "anger management in the workplace" inquiry by management or HR professionals.

REPRESSED ANGER

By contrast, people who are too afraid to assert themselves may repress angry feelings rather than think realistically about what they need to do for themselves. The repressed anger can build up and erupt against others or themselves at a later time. Anger turned against the self is a defensive strategy in which one punishes himself with anger. Some may do this to avoid getting angry at someone else. Depression is a likely outcome in any case. They may also act out by harming themselves in some way.

RESENTMENT

Resentment is anger on a low boil. It can lead to blaming, loathing, ill-will and chronic hostility. Chronic resentment primes the way for passive aggressive behavior, acting-out, and rage reactions. It also consumes one's psyche and damages health.

PASSIVE-AGGRESSIVE BEHAVIOR

Passive-aggressive behavior includes a pattern of sarcasm and deliberate emotional neglect or coldness towards loved ones.

Individuals who employ a passive-aggressive interpersonal coping strategy may avoid direct confrontations. Passive aggressive behaviors are covert and active forms of hostility. These "accidental" or stealthy forms of verbal or even physical abuse inflict harm in such a way as to provide deniability or protective cover for the aggressor. "Passive-aggressive character disorder" (or personality disorder) is not a formal psychological diagnosis. It refers to people who characteristically relate in this covertly hostile style towards at least some significant people in their life.

JUDGMENTAL ANGER

Judgmental anger consists of criticizing others at the expense of the person who is being disparaged. The goal may be to make one self feel better, or to control or damage others. The harsh criticism of righteous anger can mask malicious intentions towards the person who is being blamed while holding oneself blameless.

RETALIATORY ANGER

Retaliatory anger is a very common anger dynamic, especially in families and other close relationships. Retaliatory or payback anger is an angry reaction or response towards a person who is perceived as directing something hurtful towards one self. It is as if the target of our anger had poured something toxic into our bucket (for no valid reason that we can see). To feel better, we must "get even." So we pour the toxic feeling back into their bucket. Retaliatory anger may be automatic and or intentional. In either case, it tends to lead to a reciprocal payback cycle that keeps the problem going. Escalation can make the dynamics of reciprocal anger much worse and create an emotional vendetta.

OBSESSIVE ANGER

Obsessive anger can include paranoid fears, jealousy, envy, as well as maladaptive fears of betrayal, rejection, or humiliation. Angry obsessions can destroy one's sense of self-worth and emotional security. Seething obsessive anger creates a churning, ruminative hostility. Seething anger can set the stage for episodic, angry outbursts, rage reactions, or health problems.

RAGE

Rage is the full, uncontrolled, physical and psychological expression of the classic fight-or-flight response. Rage anger is extreme but not common for most people. It hijacks the mind and body. Rage reactions (or rage attacks) may include a sense of relief or even joy in the release of pent-up, painful feelings. When raging, control of one's social perception, judgment, speech, and motor behavior in seriously weakened. Rage attacks may be followed by selective or partial amnesia for the facts of the event. Rampage anger is a rare, extreme case of rage anger. Mini rages are less severe but happen more often, especially in intimate and family relationships.

MANIPULATIVE OR INSTRUMENTAL ANGER

Manipulative or instrumental anger is the intentional use of angry feelings or aggression in order to get one's way or to control a person or situation. Manipulative anger is dysfunctional when it is used as an emotional weapon or tool for resolving conflicts with family members, peers, and others. Ultimately, manipulative or instrumental anger is self-defeating as a long-term strategy.

OVERWHELMED OR FLOODED ANGER

Overwhelmed or flooded anger can occur when overwhelming fear, or a number of external demands or internal stressors overwhelm a person's coping ability. The overwhelmed or flooded anger reaction often resembles a temper tantrum.

IN SUMMARY

Do not be too alarmed if you experience one or more of the above types of anger behaviors. Anger problems are a matter of their degree, duration, and consequences. In any case, it is much easier to address a current or potential anger issue when we can identify and describe it clearly.

PSYCHOLOGICAL DISORDERS ACCOMPANIED BY SYMPTOMS OF ANGER

In some instances, a psychological disorder is the background condition that supports, or causes symptoms of anger. Stated another way, anger can be a symptom of a psychological condition. The following is a brief discussion of anger symptoms associated with some common psychological disorders.

INTERMITTENT EXPLOSIVE DISORDER (IED)

Intermittent Explosive Disorder (IED) is characterized by periodic eruptions of anger and rage which are disproportionate to the circumstances. Individuals with this Impulse Control Disorder are usually impulsive young men. They may threaten, assault others, harm themselves, or destroy property. These eruptions come after a period of heightened internal tension, followed by feelings of emotional release and immediate regret.

DEPRESSIVE DISORDER

In a Depressive Disorder, low mood, irritability, diminished self-esteem, reduced frustration tolerance, and heightened self-pity can create anger control problems. For men, shame plays an important role in causing depression and anger control problems. For women, concerns about abandonment, loss, and rejection tend to create depression and anger problems. To a casual observer, clinical depression will be more obvious in women than men. Men tend to under-report Depressive and Anxiety Disorders. Depression and Anxiety Disorder sufferers are often in state of tension. Their overworked nervous systems are vulnerable to hyper arousal and then exhaustion. These lower the threshold for angry reactions.

ANXIETY DISORDERS

Anxiety Disorders include Posttraumatic Stress Disorder (PTSD), Panic Disorder (panic attacks), Phobia, and Generalized Anxiety Disorder. The ruminative cognitive style in Obsessive Compulsive Disorder (OCD) is conducive to resentment. OCD sets the stage by harboring feelings jealousy, fears of abandonment, and fantasies of being disrespected, harmed, or victimized. Anxiety can prime the brain for an anger or rage event.

PERSONALITY DISORDER

Personality Disorders are characterized by rigidity and denial. Many individuals with Obsessive Compulsive Personality Disorder (OCPD) are perfectionistic, judgmental, and demanding. OCD and OCPD sufferers act as if their life depends upon attaining a particular goal or having their demands met. Individuals with Narcissistic Personality Disorder (NPD) are subject to rage reactions when their compelling need for attention or admiration is frustrated. People with Histrionic Personality Disorder are vulnerable to angry outbursts when they are emotionally flooded. People with Borderline Personality Disorder (BPD) are exceptionally vulnerable to anger due to an unstable sense of interpersonal connection and self worth. This results in roller coaster-like emotionality, rage reactions, and tenuous relationships.

SEEKING HELP

Consulting a psychologist, counselor, or psychiatrist for anger management

Are there signs of dysfunctional, aggressive behaviors, or unhealthy patterns of expressing your anger, or problems with controlling angry thoughts and feelings? Is excessive anger part of a psychological disorder or due to a difficult or stressful situation? From a practical perspective, if anger is creating significant problems for you, or for those you care about, you probably should consider consulting a mental health professional who is also an anger management specialist. An anger management consultant, who is a licensed psychologist, psychiatrist, or certified psychotherapist, can help to find the most effective solutions for you. Identifying and defining an anger problem is halfway towards solving it. Problems with anger are treatable. It may be useful to read on and learn more about the dynamics and types of treatment for dysfunctional anger issues. [www.angermanagementnyc.com/types-of-anger][1]

grace

"The grace of our Lord Jesus Christ be with you all.
Amen."

revelation chapter twenty-two verse twenty-one
[new living translation]

conclusion

happily ever after

happy

happy

happy

An excerpt from, "Mirror Mirror" by Dianne Wilson

Once upon a time, a wealthy gentleman lost his beloved wife. Grief-stricken, he remarried, but the woman he chose was very cruel and she hated his lovely daughter, Cinderella. Sadly, soon after Cinderella's father wed this hardhearted woman, he died from a broken heart. Cinderella's stepmother ordered her to live in the cellar and work with the servants. She felt so small and insignificant; she was unloved and told time and again how useless she was. Cinderella began to lose her identity as her soul became buried beneath the torment of her life.

One day, the entire community was invited to a royal ball. Cinderella's two stepsisters made a great fuss of putting on their finest clothes. After they left, Cinderella sat in a corner and wept. Suddenly, Cinderella's godmother arrived and found her precious goddaughter in a terrible state.

"I wish I could go to the ball," sobbed Cinderella.

"You shall," her godmother said, and produced the most magnificent gown, woven in the finest silk and gold, with a beautiful pair of glass slippers.

Cinderella put on the gorgeous gown and slippers and stood nervously in front of the mirror. She couldn't believe her eyes. The mirror reflected her inner beauty, love, kindness, gentleness and self-control. She saw her true self, an image she had not seen for a very long time.

Blooming with newfound confidence, it was Cinderella's turn to be a princess. There was just one condition: she had to return home before midnight, when the magnificent gown would disappear, leaving her in her familiar rags.

When Cinderella arrived at the ball, the prince was immediately drawn to this mysterious young woman and invited her to dance. They danced and danced until suddenly the clock struck twelve. Cinderella fled without even saying goodbye, and in her haste she dropped one of the glass slippers.

When Cinderella arrived home, her godmother was waiting for her. She led Cinderella back to the mirror, but Cinderella was too afraid to look — she couldn't bear to see herself in filthy rags again. When she finally opened her eyes, Cinderella saw that she was as beautiful as she had been just hours before. The mirror had captured her true reflection.

After the ball, the prince could not rest. He proclaimed that he would search the kingdom and marry the woman whose foot fitted the glass slipper. When his messengers arrived at Cinderella's home the next morning, the stepsisters tried to squeeze their feet into the slipper, but it was impossible for them. Right then, Cinderella knew she had a choice. She could keep her ragged shoes on and remain the servant, or she could dare to step into the glass slipper and into her future.

Trembling, she said, "Sir, please let me try on the slipper."

Her stepsisters and stepmother burst out laughing and mocked Cinderella, saying, "This slipper belongs to a princess." But their mockery was soon silenced as the messenger slid the slipper onto her foot and it fit her perfectly. Exchanging her rags for riches, the beautiful young woman held her head high as she walked towards her future with the handsome prince, and they lived together happily ever after.

The End.

truth

Fact

One in two marriages are ending in divorce.

Truth

Divorce doesn't have to mean dysfunction.

Cinderella is a story known to us all. It's the original rags-to-riches, Prince-Charming-to-the-rescue fairy-tale. She was a beautiful young woman downtrodden by her family dysfunction and the oppression of a nasty stepmother and stepsisters. In order to break the cycle, she had to be brave enough to step out of the mold and to see herself as the beautiful young woman she was, and she had to be willing to begin a new family life. In this instance, her godmother kindly stood her in front of a mirror to show her how truly beautiful she was — inside and out.

Cinderella chose to listen; she chose to listen to her godmother and to believe what she saw in the mirror. This empowered her to ignore the voices of the past: the negativity, criticism, ridicule and all the harsh words of her stepmother and stepsisters. She proved herself able to rise above her circumstances by turning her "stepfamily life" into "stepping stones" to her future.

The circumstances of our lives certainly have the potential to wear us down, rob us of healthy self-esteem, skew our perception of the world around us, and mess with our expectations for our future. Sometimes those challenging circumstances are ones that we were born into (such as a dysfunctional family life), or may be the result of others using their freedom against us to bring us to a place of personal brokenness. Other times we find that our challenging circumstances are brought about by poor decisions we ourselves have made over the years.

I believe that there is hope for you to have a future that is characterized by functional and healthy relationships, no matter what your past looks like, and no matter what level of dysfunction you may have been subjected to growing up.

"Faith is being sure of what we hope for and certain of what we do not yet see." [Hebrews 11:1]

In the story we just read, Cinderella faced almost insurmountable obstacles every single day. Instead of complete love and security, Cinderella's life was one of insecurity and obscurity. I can just about imagine her crying out in desperation for much needed space from the turmoil!

Our identity is challenged and rocked by going through situations that we don't think we can bear. This kind of experience takes its toll. It is in those situations that we start to compare our life with others' and sometimes even question our existence. I have felt like "a nothing" on earth. I can remember feeling like I was living a thrown away existence inside a trashcan. A trashcan with the lid down tight and a sign on the front saying, "Do not disturb." I was in so much pain that I felt I couldn't bear it. The last thing I would have ever thought at the time was that I was valuable or worth anything at all.

When our family situation or the hurt of past broken relationships bring a sense of hopelessness, we need to replace it with hopefulness. When we are feeling a sense of worthlessness, we need to take action to produce a sense of being worth something.

When you lose someone that you have cared deeply about, whether they are a mother, father, husband, wife, son or daughter, there is a desperate sense of wanting something that you cannot have. Our tendency is to remain focused on the loss and not on the future. I know what it is to experience the loss of a marriage. All I ever wanted was the "white picket fence" family; after all, that's what I had grown up with and it was all I knew.

In a perfect world there wouldn't be marriage break-up and family breakdown, but we are not living in a perfect world. Instead, many of us contend with stepfamily or single parent life, either good or bad. Each of us should be able to enjoy the security that a happy family brings. We should be able to feel safe and secure in who we are as people. Instead, when relationships experience challenges, we can go through feelings of uncertainty, comparisons, jealousy, and sibling rivalry. And these are just some of the negative results of a broken home.

Cinderella had lost her mother and became part of a blended family as a stepchild, with a stepmother and stepsisters. She then lost her father and, in his absence, she was subjected to emotional and physical abuse. She was told that she was unattractive and useless. Cinderella's self-esteem was at an all-time low. She experienced insecurity and uncertainty because she was deprived of the love and concern of a caring family. In her new family she was given no sense of purpose, future or hope. Many people can relate to the story of Cinderella.

Have the circumstances of your life caused you to feel just like Cinderella did before she entered into her happily ever after?

When you are told continually that you are worthless, that you don't have value, that you are ugly or stupid and that you will never be good for anything, you will start to believe it, especially when it is your family saying these things. I have lost count of the number of people I've met who have told me about hurtful things family members or people have said to them over and over again and eventually they began to believe what they had been told. The bad stuff is always easier to believe.

Negative emotional attacks are soul-destroying, and so too is being completely ignored. It may be that you haven't been consistently insulted, but maybe you are hardly ever noticed, spoken to, or considered. Perhaps you feel as though you are so unimportant that no one would notice or care if you weren't around any more. That is just not true! That is a lie that has entered your life in order to destroy it.

Please believe the truth that you are valuable, important and that you have hope and a future. The story of Cinderella represents people today who have a number of issues to deal with, both in their family situation and personally, which affects their self-esteem, among other things. We need to find out who we really are and why on earth we were born.

I am happy to be an optimist, and I am optimistic enough to believe that we have the power to change our lives, regardless of our circumstances.

I believe that we reach a certain age or level of maturity that requires us to no longer blame our parents or ex-spouse for the mess in which we may find our family lives. Blame casting only keeps us bound in dysfunction and misery. We need to recognize the dysfunction around us and then take responsibility for our own lives. That's how we discover the truth and break the cycle.

You may have found yourself "in motion" as part of a non-traditional family, but it doesn't mean that you are necessarily part of a dysfunctional family. And if there are elements of your family that seem like they don't work or are dysfunctional, you can break the cycle by taking responsibility for and focusing on the truth of your life and making it functional. Living in denial does nothing to help change our present or our future. Once we face the facts, we can then search for the truth and find a solution that will bring freedom to our lives.

I believe you have the ability to rise above your circumstances and become all that you were created to be, regardless of how dysfunctional your family life may have been in the past or may be currently.

NEW BEGINNINGS

I believe that the happily ever after life of freedom is available to all, regardless of the family situation in which you may find yourself. We all need someone to help us see ourselves as we really are. Just as Cinderella stood in front of a mirror and finally saw the truth, we sometimes need a mirror, such as this book, to reflect the truth about our potential, not just the facts about the problems we may be facing.

Problems don't just disappear, they need to be worked through and solved. The key to a life of freedom and a brighter future is to recognize what you cannot change, and learn to live a great life by changing what you can.

Many people who have had a traditional family life, only to lose it and begin again, have to face some immense obstacles. In order to conquer these obstacles they can't afford to feel sorry for themselves or take on the woe-is-me-bitter-forever syndrome. The power of forgiveness plays a significant part in the healing and growing process. We have to release the power of forgiveness over our family (yes, those who have caused us grief), in order to move forward. This requires us to forgive them regardless of their response and show one-way love. Forgiving others is the catalyst that sets us free. Forgiving others not only releases others of their debt to us, but it releases us from holding onto resentment or hatred that hurts us and damages our identity.

You can make whatever you want of your life if you allow forgiveness and healing to take place. We need to forgive others who have hurt us. Please don't allow labels or any other "boxes" to trap you into a life of containment, a life boxed in your past. You are not defined by your marital, parental or family status. You are defined by who you are as a human being. If I had to rely on marriage for my identity and self-esteem, I would still be living a sad and broken life, because my first marriage ended, and I wouldn't be in a healthy enough state to build another marriage the second time around.

Some of us need the fairy tale. Without it, we might believe that life will inevitably be lived in the cellar. We can have the fairy tale when we allow the reality in our lives to be overlaid by the happily ever after life story. Have faith for the story to become your reality.

This is not the end of the story. One door may have closed in your life, but you can be sure, as you search, another door will be opened.

272 BOYS, GUYS & MEN by Dianne Wilson

In Christ, you can find hope for the future, and healing in areas of brokenness or places of grief.

As you entrust all your relationships to God moving forward, and ask Him for help and wisdom, you will find that He'll show you how best to move forward in each one. God restores, heals and delivers. Your best days are indeed ahead of you!

Perhaps you have never experienced relational dysfunction, or heartache. I pray that you will continue to walk in wholeness and freedom, exercising wisdom that you have picked up from the mistakes that others have made, so that you don't have to make them yourself! Remember who you are and who God has called you to be. You are a merchant ship and you carry the purpose of God. Choose wisely!

Just as the author of the original Cinderella penned the ending to be happily ever after, you have the opportunity to write your own ending to your life story. It's up to you. This is not the end of the story. One door may have closed in your life, but you can be sure, as you search, another door will be opened.

The Happily Ever After end to my story is truly miraculous. My relationship with my former husband has become more respectful and more gracious with each passing year. He and his wife and daughter moved closer to us and they see the boys often as well as coming to our church every week. We enjoy birthdays, Thanksgiving and Christmas together as a family. It may not be conventional, but it is one of great grace. Remember the Truth: divorce doesn't have to mean dysfunction. Functional people make functional families, and dysfunctional people make dysfunctional families. Our ability to be functional is everything. The word functional means, "the ability to adapt." When we can adapt to whatever happens in life, by the grace of God, we can see our lives blossom and grow.

May you have great success, and flourish in every relationship and may the last words in the Word of God be ever with you.

love

"A true love story never ends."

Jesus

end notes

1. Matthew Henry, Matthew Henry's Commentary on the Whole Bible, Volume I (Genesis to Deuteronomy), Notes on Genesis 2:21–25 [Public Domain]
2. Matthew Henry, "Proverbs 31", Matthew Henry's Concise Commentary on the Bible, [Public Domain]

INTRODUCTION | BOYS GUYS MEN
1. Dr Phil McGraw, Life Law #8: http://www.drphil.com/articles/article/44
2. Lord Byron, Don Juan, Canto XIV, 101; The Major Works, ed. Jerome J. McGann [Oxford: Oxford University Press, 2000]
3. Eleanor Roosevelt, Book of Common Sense Etiquette, Macmillan, 1962

PART ONE | TRUE STORY
1. Robert Sapolsky, Biology and Human Behavior: The Neurological Origins of Individuality, 2nd edition [2005].

CHAPTER ONE | THE DATING YEARS
1. Leonardo da Vinci. BrainyQuote.com, Xplore Inc, 2014. http://www.brainyquote.com/quotes/quotes/l/leonardoda120051.html, accessed September 23, 2014.

CHAPTER TWO | THE SILENT YEARS
1. Plato. BrainyQuote.com, Xplore Inc, 2014. http://www.brainyquote.com/quotes/quotes/p/plato403317.html, accessed September 23, 2014.
2. Benjamin Franklin. BrainyQuote.com, Xplore Inc, 2014. http://www.brainyquote.com/quotes/quotes/b/benjaminfr123487.html, accessed September 23, 2014.

CHAPTER THREE | THE BABY YEARS
1. John Newton, Amazing Grace, First published 1779, Public Domain

CHAPTER FOUR | THE GRACE YEARS
1. Henry Ward Beecher. BrainyQuote.com, Xplore Inc, 2014. http://www.brainyquote.com/quotes/quotes/h/henrywardb165303.html, accessed September 24, 2014.

CHAPTER FIVE | THE FOREVER YEARS
1. Rainer Maria Rilke. BrainyQuote.com, Xplore Inc, 2014.
http://www.brainyquote.com/quotes/quotes/r/rainermari393352.html, accessed
September 24, 2014.

PART TWO | BOYS, GUYS, MEN
1. Randy Pausch, Jeffrey Zaslow, The Last Lecture, Hodder & Stoughton, 2008 [reprint]
2. Phil McGraw, Newsweek, Volume 140, Newsweek, Incorporated, 2002

CHAPTER SEVEN | SEVEN SIGNS THAT HE IS MR WRONG
1. Kin Hubbard. BrainyQuote.com, Xplore Inc, 2014.
http://www.brainyquote.com/quotes/quotes/k/kinhubbard106733.html, accessed
September 25, 2014.
2. Mahatma Gandhi. BrainyQuote.com, Xplore Inc, 2014.
http://www.brainyquote.com/quotes/quotes/m/mahatmagan160799.html, accessed
September 29, 2014.

CHAPTER EIGHT | FIVE TIME BOMBS THAT MAY DESTROY A
RELATIONSHIP
1. Natalie Wood. BrainyQuote.com, Xplore Inc, 2014.
http://www.brainyquote.com/quotes/quotes/n/nataliewoo106759.html, accessed
September 24, 2014.

CHAPTER NINE | EIGHT QUALITIES TO LOOK FOR IN A LIFE PARTNER
1. Antoine de Saint-Exupery. BrainyQuote.com, Xplore Inc, 2014.
http://www.brainyquote.com/quotes/quotes/a/antoinedes154901.html, accessed
September 24, 2014.

PART THREE | GIRLS, CHICKS, WOMEN

CHAPTER ELEVEN | BOUNDARIES
1. Dr Henry Cloud & Dr John Townsend, Boundaries, Zondervan Publishing House,
Michigan 1992
2. Louis de Bernieres, Captain Corelli's Mandolin, Random House 2011
3. Thomas Merton. BrainyQuote.com, Xplore Inc, 2014.
http://www.brainyquote.com/quotes/quotes/t/thomasmert121801.html, accessed
September 25, 2014.

CHAPTER TWELVE | THE LEAN OF FAITH
1. Epicurus. BrainyQuote.com, Xplore Inc, 2014.
http://www.brainyquote.com/quotes/quotes/e/epicurus119456.html, accessed
September 24, 2014.

CHAPTER THIRTEEN | HEY LITTLE GIRL

1. Michael J. Fox. BrainyQuote.com, Xplore Inc, 2014.
http://www.brainyquote.com/quotes/quotes/m/michaeljf189284.html, accessed
September 25, 2014.

CHAPTER FOURTEEN | THE MISTRESS

1. Liz Curtis Higgs: http://www.lizcurtishiggs.com/bad-girls-of-the-bible-the-sinful-woman/, published 11/06/13. Used with permission. All rights reserved.

ANGER MANAGEMENT

1. Robert M. Fraum, PhD, Licensed Psychologist:
www.angermanagementnyc.com/types-of-anger